DIGITAL DEFENSE

DIGITAL DEFENSE

What You Should Know About
Protecting Your Company's Assets

THOMAS J. PARENTY

HARVARD BUSINESS SCHOOL PRESS
BOSTON, MASSACHUSETTS

Copyright 2003 Harvard Business School Publishing Corporation

All rights reserved

Printed in the United States of America

07 06 05 04 03   5 4 3 2 1

Some of the methods and systems in this book may be covered by one or more of the following patent applications: WO 02/43317 and U.S. 2002/0064283; and, may also be covered by other U.S. and foreign patents or patent applications. It is the responsibility of the reader to obtain all necessary patent licenses before implementing any methods or producing any systems in this book. This book does not contain an exhaustive list of all applicable patents or patent applications.

TRANSPARENT KEY MANAGEMENT™ is a trademark owned by Parenty Consulting, LLC.

Requests for permission to use or reproduce material from this book should be directed to permissions@hbsp.harvard.edu, or mailed to Permissions, Harvard Business School Publishing, 60 Harvard Way, Boston, Massachusetts 02163.

The author is in no way affiliated with Digital Defense, Inc., of San Antonio, Texas.

Library of Congress Cataloging-in-Publication Data

Parenty, Thomas J.
Digital defense : what you should know about protecting
your company's assets / Thomas J. Parenty.
p. cm.
ISBN 1-57851-779-6 (alk. paper)
1. Business enterprises—Computer networks—Security measures.
2. Electronic commerce—Security measures.
3. Computer security. 4. Data protection. I. Title.
HD30.38.P37 2003
658.4'78—dc21
2003002450

The paper used in this publication meets the requirements of the American National Standard for Permanence of Paper for Publications and Documents in Libraries and Archives Z39.48-1992.

*To my professors at Holy Cross
who taught me how to think and to
David Bell who taught me how to
think about security.*

CONTENTS

ACKNOWLEDGMENTS

The process of writing this book entailed reevaluating all of what I've known or believed about information security for the past twenty years. This meant reexamining numerous information security technologies, their effectiveness, and their relevance in today's business world. Although I was relieved to find that much of what I've held to be true all these years stood up to scrutiny, there were many cases in which I realized my understanding only went so far and that there were issues I hadn't fully grasped or considered. Fortunately, numerous friends and colleagues helped me to deepen and hone my understanding of what really matters in information security and why. I could not have written this book without their help and insight. To those who are not listed here, please accept my apologies for the omission and my gratitude for your assistance.

In particular, I'm grateful to Steve Beason, Bill Crowell, Y. Jay Jayachandra, John Sebes, and Nanjunda Somayaji for their help in developing the fundamental themes and objectives of the book. I'm thankful to Steve Burchell, Dave Ferraiolo, Fabrice Guérini, Karen Hogoboom, Dave Neudoerffer, Laura Olson, Charles Pfleeger, Ed Roback, Rena Tom, Tom Wills, Steve Zamek, and Ed Zeitler for sharing with me their information technology and security experience.

Joe Keegan and Susan Kwong were always available when I needed a quick technical answer (or a sanity check), and Gary Truax spent many hours with me reviewing and discussing initial drafts. Dennis Brown, Dee Elling, and Beverley Farmes provided perspectives on corporate security practices and the use of security features in enterprise applications. Joseph Alhadeff, Romy Celli, Lisa Kinard, Charles Merrill, and Melissa Waksman provided insight into legal and policy issues, and Louise Sully Mintun and Bob Staples clarified the prudent ways in which investment professionals distribute and evaluate stock information on the Internet. Ron Morgan helped me to understand issues facing corporate human resource departments, and Everett Crosby researched medieval precedents for online user credentials.

Throughout the writing process, Lisa Welchman helped me to clarify my thoughts, checked the soundness of my reasoning, and encouraged me. Mickey Butts provided valuable editorial assistance during the formative stages of the book, and Sharon Alger's encouragement and understanding during the last six months of writing, as well as her comments on the book's content, were a huge support.

I am indebted to Fred Chang, John Chen, Kevin Cornish, Jack Domet, Abe Sofaer, and Bill Wilson for reviewing complete drafts. Their suggestions and charitable criticisms improved the book. Talking with Terry Anderson, Armistead Maupin, and Roger Wieck about the process of writing helped me immeasurably. Learning that I'm not the only author who has taken thirteen hours to write three hundred words was quite a consolation.

Organizing and presenting the material in this book in a way that could be understood by someone who is not already a security expert was a significant challenge, and one that I could have accomplished only with Debbie Williamson's help. Debbie's editorial focus on clarity was invaluable and much appreciated, even when it meant I had to rewrite some sections half a dozen times.

The entire staff at Harvard Business School Press, including Astrid Sandoval and Hollis Heimbouch, has been a joy to work with and has made my first book publishing experience better than I could have hoped for.

My final and most important acknowledgment is to my editor at HBS Press, Suzanne Rotondo, who got me involved in all of this by suggesting that I write a book in the first place. She guided me from the initial proposal phase through a year and a half of writing, taking time off only to give birth to her daughter. As my friend, Suzanne provided the encouragement I needed to work on the most demanding project of my life; as my editor, she provided the direction I needed to complete it.

INTRODUCTION

Every day, new stories of viruses, hacker attacks, and security gaffes flood the news media. In the first half of 2002, 3,279 new viruses infected computers around the world, according to antivirus software company Sophos.[1] Meanwhile, high-profile denial-of-service attacks against prominent Web sites such as eBay and Yahoo! have prompted Congressional hearings.[2] Everywhere you look, it seems, the seamy underbelly of the computer world is out to get you. You could spend countless dollars buying the latest technology to defend against every possible attack. But that strategy is always two steps behind. No matter how many attacks you fend off, there's always one that you didn't expect.

Over the past twenty years, I have advised numerous companies and government organizations on information security, and I've seen many of them make grave security mistakes. One company stores and manages sensitive business and financial information for its customers. Given that many of this company's customers compete with each other, this firm went to great lengths to make sure that no one would be able to access a customer's information except for that customer. Unfortunately, all of this company's security efforts focused on protecting against attacks coming in through the front door. The company didn't examine its own back-office operations, which included sending all of the sensitive information from clients to an overseas supplier whose job was to put all of the data into a standard format.

There was no protection for this information while it traveled over the Internet between the company and the overseas supplier, nor were there any security mechanisms to protect the information while it was at the supplier's site.

In another instance, a brokerage firm with operations in more than forty countries decided to upgrade the information security protections for the systems its employees use to perform financial transactions on behalf of clients. This brokerage firm purchased state-of-the-art-technology to identify employees when they logged on and to keep detailed records of every action their employees took. The technology followed the model of using a passport, in which an official checks both that the passport is valid and that it belongs to the person presenting it. The security vendor that sold this authentication technology went to great lengths to make sure the "passports" employees presented while logging on were valid. However, the vendor neglected to make sure a passport actually belonged to the employee presenting it. If this security flaw had not been discovered and fixed before the brokerage firm installed the software, any employee at this firm could, with no hacking skills and with little difficulty, impersonate any other employee at the firm. Once the impersonation began, all of the actions of the rogue employee would have been attributed to someone else.

Both companies thought they were doing the right thing. They took action to fix security problems, but they didn't go far enough. In these and many other situations, the security holes were invisible to the companies, but left them perilously close to disaster.

WHY ADDRESS SECURITY?

Why should businesses address information security, and why is it important to do so in a comprehensive way? One answer is risk management. Attacks on corporate computers and the theft and misuse of corporate information pose risks that responsible businesses need to assess and manage. Guarding against information security breaches carries the same fiscal responsibility as protecting a company's physical assets.

However, there is another reason why businesses should take a second and harder look at information security: the critical role it plays in transforming the way businesses operate and in opening up new business opportunities. Consider the film industry. Producing a feature film involves massive amounts of sensitive information, from film and soundtrack clips to financing and marketing plans. Individuals working around the globe need access to this information, and it must be shared securely and conveniently. The current practice for distributing "dailies," the results of a day's filming, involves couriers and overnight delivery services. With the right information security protections in place, dailies could be sent instantly over the Internet to everyone who needs them, regardless of their location, resulting in a substantial increase in efficiency and flexibility. This could shorten decision-making time, facilitate collaboration, and compress filming schedules.

Today, most businesses consider information security a reactionary position, not an enabling technology. A flurry of security activity often follows an attack, such as a virus or a Web site crash. Companies also address security to avoid the pain of noncompliance with government regulations. The financial services and health care industries have paid close attention to information security to meet government regulations, since regulators can force a company that doesn't comply to close its doors.

The common theme across all of these approaches is that while they address immediate security concerns, they are defensive tactics that fail to address the larger role information security should play in today's business environment.

Businesses increasingly rely on the secure use and sharing of digital, or computer-based, information to operate competitively and grow. This digital information includes a wide range of business assets, such as engineering diagrams for a new automobile engine, the terms of a proposed corporate acquisition, or the destination account number for an electronic funds transfer. This dependence on the reliability and security of digital information is not limited to companies born on the Internet, such as online music and bookstores or Internet stock trading firms. Every company that uses computers to manage some part of its business—even if it doesn't use the Internet at all—needs to worry about information security. Even companies that don't have computers in-house need to be concerned, because the security of the digital information managed by companies with whom they do business affects them as well.

WHO SHOULD READ THIS BOOK

This book addresses the needs of businesspeople who recognize the importance of protecting their company's critical information assets. It is designed to help managers understand the powerful relationship between information security and their organization's growth strategy.

Information security isn't just the domain of the information technology (IT) department. Because senior management is responsible for ensuring the ongoing health and success of a company, understanding the impact of information security practices and policies is paramount. Information security also plays a role in developing new products, expanding to new markets, and improving operational efficiency. Businesspeople need to understand the information security protections their future plans need, as well as the future plans information security can enable.

Although this book focuses on the information security issues facing businesses, the concepts and practices discussed here are directly applicable to government and nonprofit organizations as well. All enterprises need to address information security in a comprehensive way, and the processes for doing this are largely the same. The fundamental security issues surrounding the sharing of sensitive information between different companies are the same as those for sharing sensitive information between different government organizations.

THE ROLE OF TRUST

This book introduces a unique approach for developing and implementing a corporate security process. This approach to information security is based on two principles. The first is that any effective corporate security process has to be closely linked to the *specific* business activities and mission of the company. All measures to secure a company's information and systems that are not based on an understanding of what a company does are inherently incomplete because they can only protect against generic attacks on a company's computers.

The second principle is that *trust* is an essential component of all business activities. You need to know what to trust so that a business activity can meet its objective, and you need to know what evidence is required to establish that trust. This has been prudent business practice since the beginning of commerce.

In the early fifteenth century, for example, the Chinese merchant fleet, under the direction of Admiral Zheng He, made extensive trading voyages throughout the East and South China Seas, the Indian Ocean, and the Persian Gulf.[3] In order to accomplish their business objectives of increased wealth and influence, government officials and merchants knew that they needed to trust that the contents of their treasure ships were safe from theft or damage. The warships, patrol boats, and tens of thousands of soldiers and sailors that escorted the treasure ships provided the necessary evidence to establish this trust. When undertaking any business activity, you need to understand what must be trusted to accomplish your business objectives, and what it takes to establish this trust. You need a Trust Framework.

The Trust Framework is built on two elements: trust objectives and trust evidence.

- *Trust objectives* are the security attributes of a business activity— for example, a corporate merger or sale of a product—that a businessperson or company must believe are true in order to be confident that the activity can succeed and accomplish its business objectives. Examples of trust objectives include being sure that a business partner is who he says he is, keeping sensitive business information secret, and having an official record of a business transaction. Trust objectives are the same in the digital and non-digital worlds.

- *Trust evidence* provides the proof necessary for a businessperson or company to believe that the trust objective has been met. In the non-digital world, trust evidence is often obvious. An introduction by a mutual colleague is a common form of trust evidence for establishing the identity of a new business partner. Sending a document via registered mail or a bonded delivery service provides the necessary evidence for keeping sensitive information secret in most cases, and paper receipts provide evidence of completed business transactions. But as business operations move to the digital world, these common forms of evidence disappear.

The role of information security technology within the Trust Framework is to provide the necessary evidence to meet a company's trust objectives in the digital world. It provides the reasons why a businessperson trusts that the partner he has communicated with only via e-mail is who he claims to be, why he trusts that the sensitive document he sent over the Internet won't fall into the hands of a competitor, and why he trusts that the partner can't repudiate an online business transaction after the fact.

This is a significantly different approach to security from one centered on technologies such as firewalls and virus protection. Those technologies focus on securing a company's computers and networks. In contrast, the security process described in this book focuses on the fundamental issue of securing a company's business activities and information. The process includes the use of technologies such as firewalls, but always in the context of a company's business objectives.

The value of the Trust Framework extends beyond its role in helping companies select information security technology. When a company defines its trust objectives for a business activity, it is making an explicit statement about what security means for that activity. By linking its selection of information security technologies and procedures to its trust objectives, a company offers explicit evidence of how it is making a business activity secure.

Only with this information can a business accurately assess and manage the risks associated with its online business activities. Furthermore, only with this information can potential business partners, customers, and government regulators gauge the safety of conducting business with a company. By contrast, knowing that a company has a firewall and uses virus protection doesn't provide any meaningful information about how safe it is to conduct business with that firm over the Internet.

This direct linkage between trust objectives and security technology also provides a quick answer to the question of why a company is spending time and money on an information security solution. If a company can't tie a security solution back to a business trust objective, it probably shouldn't be using that solution.

BUILDING A BETTER CORPORATE SECURITY PROCESS

The structure of this book mirrors the process of evaluating a company's information security requirements and deploying solutions to meet those requirements over time. The first few chapters discuss the initial steps of the corporate security process and traditional approaches to computer security. The middle of the book lays out the Trust Framework and the four main trust objectives, and the information security technologies that provide evidence that those objectives have been met. The last two chapters provide guidance for companies on organizational issues associated with implementing a comprehensive corporate security process, and on using the Trust Framework to identify and pursue new business opportunities. Appendix B contains a diagram that guides companies through the entire process.

1. Identifying Your Information Assets

The first step in protecting your company's information assets is to identify them. Assets can take the form of electronic versions of paper documents, or data that control automated functions, such as package routing. Once you've identified the assets you want to protect, you need to prioritize them based on their value to your company.

2. Determining Your Current Vulnerabilities

First, look at all the information assets that your existing security solutions allow users to access. Then, assume the role of a hacker and look at all the subversive ways an outsider could gain access to company information. The combination of both perspectives provides a full picture of the current vulnerabilities facing your company's sensitive business information.

3. Protecting Your Computers

Security technologies such as virus protection, intrusion detection, networking monitoring, and firewalls are important, but they don't address the protection of specific corporate information assets. Chapter 3 provides a brief discussion of these technologies and explains how they fit within the overall corporate security process.

4. Developing a Security Process Based on Trust

Look at information security technology in a new light. Determine what your company needs to trust in any given business activity and select information security technologies based on their ability to establish this trust in the digital world.

5. Keeping Information Confidential

The first trust objective addresses the need for a private environment in which to conduct business and the importance of protecting the confidentiality of sensitive business information. Encryption can provide companies with the privacy and confidentiality they need.

6. Establishing Identity

Without knowing who a company's partners, suppliers, or customers are, virtually all business transactions would be impossible. Chapter 6 explains how companies can create and authenticate digital identities to establish trust in their online partners.

7. Controlling Access in the Digital World

The value a company derives from its information assets depends on the company's ability to deliver information to the right people while preventing the wrong people from accessing it. Chapter 7 covers information security options, such as controlling access by job function or role.

8. Knowing What's Real in Cyberspace

Written documents and signatures have traditionally provided companies with reliable business records. In a digital business environment, these reliable records don't exist. This final trust objective chapter addresses how companies can use security technologies such as auditing and encryption to create reliable electronic records.

9. Putting Your Security Process into Action

Protecting company information assets entails organizational issues as well as technological obstacles. These include getting senior executives to buy in, budgeting, and building a security team. Companies also need to think about how they can incorporate information security awareness into everyday business decisions.

10. Transforming Your Business Through Information Security

Once a company has addressed its current information security requirements, the next step is to explore the new business opportunities it can pursue with the right information security support. The world today is full of examples of business activities, from online shopping to the distribution of movies to theaters, that information security makes possible. The Trust Framework can help companies identify new opportunities of their own.

An entirely new era of information security is underway. Information security technology appears complex, and the void between a business function, such as selling a product, and a security mechanism, such as encryption, can seem quite large. The good news is that although the pace of technology change continues to increase, the fundamental information security issues facing businesses remain constant. Moreover, businesses were addressing these issues long before computers existed. It all comes down to trust: Determine what needs to be trusted in a business activity, and then make sure that an acceptable basis for that trust exists.

DIGITAL
DEFENSE

ONE

Identifying Your Information Assets

Before you can protect your company's sensitive information, you have to know what it is you want to protect. The first step in the corporate security process is to identify and prioritize information assets. This procedure lays the groundwork for the rest of the security process and works equally well for companies that have never formally addressed their information security needs and for those with active security programs in place. To explain how the process works, this chapter introduces a hypothetical company. This company will appear throughout the book to help illustrate how to apply the corporate security process and the Trust Framework to protect a company's valuable assets.

WHY INFORMATION ISN'T SAFE

There are two emerging trends in business and information technology that make a comprehensive corporate security process a priority. The first trend is the elimination of middlemen when routing information from a company to a person. Today, someone can place a request for a frequent flier account balance using a wireless PDA (personal digital assistant) and get the information without ever involving another person. Before, such a request would have involved contacting an employee at the airline. This human intermediary, among other things, provides an additional security check to make sure that information goes only to people who should get it. Without a human in the loop, there's no opportunity to recover from a security problem anywhere along the path.

The second trend is that companies increasingly are sharing sensitive business information in the course of pursuing new business opportunities or making existing business relationships more efficient and profitable. Consider, for example, joint product development and online purchasing. These evolving business practices place a company's sensitive information at even greater risk. This means that companies need to expand the scope of their information security concerns and protections beyond their corporate walls. They need to revise their security perspective from a model of "us against them," in which a company barricades itself from outside attacks, to one of controlled collaboration that allows secure sharing of information across company lines.

TYPES OF INFORMATION ASSETS

So what information assets must companies identify? All of the sensitive and critical business information stored and processed on computers and networks. What that means is that companies should look at three information types:

- electronic equivalents of paper documents;

- information used to control computerized processes; and

- information used by a company, but not under its direct control.

Electronic equivalents of paper documents include financial spreadsheets, marketing requirements documents, and product design specifications. One characteristic of this type of information asset is that it can be printed, and the printed version has the same value, sensitivity, and usefulness as the electronic version.

Information used to control computerized processes might include, for instance, the range of motion for an automobile assembly robot or how much water flows through a hydraulic dam gate. This type of information differs from the previous type in that a printed copy has less value than the electronic version. For example, a printout of the computer instructions for a robot arm can't make a robot do anything. This information can control a robot only when it is inside the robot's computer.

Companies can have information assets that include features of these two types. The formulas for house paint and prescription medications are two examples. Printed copies of the formulas are valuable both to the companies themselves and to their competitors. In addition, the electronic versions of these formulas can be used in automated manufacturing.

The final type of information asset is information that is not under a company's own control. In many situations, such as outsourced production, third-party sales channels, and joint product development, other organizations will have a company's sensitive information on their own computers. Even though a company does not have the same control over another company's information security protections as it does its own, it's important to account for these external information assets.

WHERE TO LOOK FOR ASSETS

With a basic understanding of what information assets are, the next question is where to look for them. The key is to take advantage of existing logical groups of information, thus breaking the task into manageable pieces.

Companies should exploit two groupings in particular: enterprise applications and collections of files on a computer. Enterprise applications such as database management systems and sales force automation manage large collections of company information, so they provide a good starting point. A sales force automation application, for example, manages information about customers and prospects, such as contact information, product support issues, and pending proposals. Employees in departments such as marketing, customer service, and sales use the application to access the information they need in order to do their jobs. The other grouping, collections of files on a computer, includes assets that are shared by employees who work together regularly or collaborate on projects.

The next challenge a company faces is determining how big an information asset is—its granularity. Is an asset all the information on an individual computer? Is it all of the files in a specific directory? Is it all of the information stored within a specific enterprise application— for example, sales force automation? Is it an individual file? Is it a specific field, such as a credit card number, on a purchase order?

The way to decide if the granularity of an asset is correct is to ask two questions. In the case of a patient's hospital record, for example, you might first ask, Is there anyone who should have access to one part of this asset, such as insurance information, who should not have access to another part, such as the patient's laboratory results? The next question you would ask is, Are the people who are allowed to access this patient record also always allowed to access other patient records? If the answer to both questions is no, then the granularity is correct. If the answer to the first question is yes, then the information asset should be divided into smaller assets until the answer to that question is no. If the answer to the second question is yes, then assets that can always be accessed by the same people can be combined into a single asset.

THE INFORMATION ASSET TABLE

Compiling a list of information assets helps focus a company's attention on what it needs to do to protect itself in a computerized and networked world. The vague goal of protecting a company transforms into the actionable goal of protecting its information assets. In addition, a list of information assets is the beginning of an information asset table, a powerful tool for managing the security process. In this table, each row is an information asset and each column contains different information about the asset that will help companies protect and manage it. Table 1-1 defines the table elements and provides an overview of the process. The table elements will be introduced over several chapters. In table 1-2, for instance, the first column lists the asset's name; the second column describes an asset's value, which helps companies prioritize their security efforts. The third column contains the department or group with business responsibility for the asset. Other columns that will be introduced later in the book include the application managing an asset, how a user logs on in order to access an asset, and whether an asset is encrypted while it is stored.

A company should maintain its information asset table electronically, such as within a database management system. That makes it easy to find all of the information about an asset or group of assets and find all of the assets that have some characteristic in common, such as high value.

TABLE 1-1

Information Asset Table: Definition of Terms

Column	Description
Name	Unique name for information asset
Value	An informal ranking of an information asset's value
Owner	The department with business ownership for the asset
Application	The application that enforces access control over asset
Current permissions	Who currently has permission to access an asset
Available permissions	All of the possible access permissions for an asset
Storage encryption	Is the asset encrypted while stored?
Current authentication	Authentication evidence currently used to access asset
Available authentication	Available authentication evidence to access an asset
Other required security technologies	Additional security technologies required to protect asset

TABLE 1-2

Information Asset Table: Name, Value, and Owner

Asset Name	Value	Owner
Term sheet for corporate acquisition	High	Executive staff
Customer record	Medium	Sales
Company phone book	Low	Human Resources (HR)

WHAT IS AN ASSET WORTH?

The information asset table will help companies take the next step in the process: determining which assets need to be protected first, second, third, and so on. One criterion for ranking assets is value. To assess the value of information, consider the damage to a company, as well as the benefits to competitors, that would result from the improper disclosure, use, or modification of an asset. Here are a few examples of how to approach the task of calculating financial damage.

A bank places value on the digital records used to execute electronic funds transfers (EFTs). A basic approximation of the value of this type of information asset is the dollar amount of the transfer. A pharmaceutical company places value on the formula for a new medicine. An approximation of the value of that information asset is the profit the company can realize from the medicine. An automobile factory places value on the computer programs that control the robots on its assembly line. The loss of revenue associated with an idle assembly line is one way of calculating that value.

The real damage that could result from not protecting these assets, however, can greatly exceed the immediate value in question. For example, fraudulent EFTs can cost a bank much more than their actual dollar amount if one considers the costs of detecting and stopping the fraud, as well as the cost of lost customers and the damage to the bank's reputation if the fraud becomes public. The inability to deliver a drug to market on time can have a long-term negative effect on the growth of a pharmaceutical company. A stalled assembly line can cause disruptions in just-in-time supply chains both backward and forward on the chain, resulting in financial losses for many companies besides the automobile manufacturer.

Since an information asset's monetary value may not be immediately apparent, one way of finding high-value assets is to look at core business functions and the information assets they use. For example, package tracking information is essential for an overnight delivery service and laboratory research notes are crucial for a pharmaceutical company.

Although assigning value to information assets is important, it's not necessary to make it a highly quantitative and complex process. An asset's value is used to make two security decisions: deciding when a company will take steps to protect an asset, and determining how much protection an asset needs. For most companies, the timing choices are now, later, or never. Information security protection options are similarly limited. Assets won't have any better protection, nor will a company reduce any real risk, by using a complex valuation process.

PUTTING IT ALL TOGETHER

Every company's information security needs are different, and the decisions firms make concerning the protection of their information assets differ as well. Still, it's helpful to know how a company navigates this terrain. Unfortunately, companies are loath to discuss any of their security protections publicly, so this book will use a composite company, ACME, to illustrate how the entire security process could work. All of the business situations ACME faces and the information security decisions it makes are derived from real-world examples.

ACME manufactures and sells products for commercial use and has annual revenues of approximately $850 million. It has been in business for twenty-five years, has operations in ten countries, and employs a workforce of approximately four thousand employees and contractors. ACME's headquarters is in the United States, and it has four manufacturing facilities and fifteen sales offices within the United States and abroad. Internally, it is structured along the following departments: research and development (R&D), manufacturing, shipping and distribution, marketing, sales, human resources, finance, business development, strategic planning, and IT.

Several developments over the course of a few months have led ACME to begin a security review of its operations. One was a memo from the general counsel saying that ACME needed to ensure that its method of processing and protecting employee health care and medical insurance information was in compliance with new government regulations. Another factor was a partnership ACME has with another company to develop a component for one of ACME's products. The R&D department had never before conducted joint development with an outside firm and was concerned about trade secrets leaking to competitors. A third factor was a virus infection that took three days for the IT department to clear up. In light of all these situations, the chief information officer (CIO) proposes to the CEO and others in senior management that ACME undertake a comprehensive assessment of the company's overall information security protection. With their approval, the CIO forms a team that will gather information on ACME's business operations, the information assets these operations use, and their protection requirements. Team members will work closely with managers and staff throughout ACME during this initial information gathering task as well as the rest of the corporate security process.

Here's how the information asset identification process works in three different departments at ACME: sales, a foreign manufacturing facility, and the R&D department.

Identifying Sales Information Assets

To save time and money, ACME doesn't plan to examine all of its sales offices. Instead, it decides to look at the two largest offices now and to schedule reviews of the other sales offices over the next two quarters.

One security team member starts by talking with the VP of sales to get a broad understanding of how the sales organization operates and its future direction. The security team member also has discussions with sales representatives and other sales department staff.

The first set of identified information assets comes from a sales force automation application, which contains information about ACME's prospects and customers. ACME decides to set the granularity of information assets within the sales force automation application to the level of individual fields within a customer record. Fortunately, the application enforces this level of granularity. The second set of assets includes information that sales reps use to close deals, including product information and competitive analyses from the marketing department. Some of this information is generally available, some is shared only with a customer under a nondisclosure agreement (NDA), and some information is never released outside of the company. Other information assets include white papers, presentations, and sales contracts that sales reps create for specific customers. These information assets are stored in a directory on a computer in the sales department.

The basis for valuing each type of sales information asset is the degree of damage a competitor could inflict on ACME's sales if the competitor could access that information. For example, a description of a product that has not yet been released is a high-value information asset. A sales rep can use this asset to close a deal, thus providing value to ACME. But this same information asset in the hands of a competitor could result in a lost sale, thus eliminating value to ACME.

Identifying Information Assets in a Factory

The second example of identifying information assets takes place in a factory, and the analysis process for this situation is the same as for the sales office. The factory uses an inventory management application to keep track of outstanding orders, raw materials, and completed products. By managing these information assets, the factory can quickly fulfill orders and minimize inventory expenses at the same time.

The machines within the factory can be configured to operate in different ways. For example, a machine can cut and bend sheet metal into different shapes and sizes. The parameters—which are information assets—that tell the machine how to process the sheet metal are downloaded from computers at corporate headquarters. In addition, IT computer operators at headquarters can remotely perform maintenance on all of the computers within the factory. This includes the ability to start and stop computers and applications as well as change the parameters that factory floor machines use to do their job. The instructions these operators send to the factory's computers, including the ones inside machines, are examples of information assets.

Within the factory, the first type of information asset supports efficient factory operation through tracking orders and inventory, among other things. These information assets are important because they save ACME money through increased efficiency. The second type of information asset controls the physical functioning of the factory and its ability to produce products. These assets have a higher value because their misuse or corruption could result in damaged equipment and supplies or even a factory shutdown.

Identifying R&D Assets

In the third example, the R&D department is working on an upgrade for one of the company's products. This upgrade includes the development of a smaller, lightweight motor, a project the R&D department has outsourced to a company that specializes in small motor design and manufacture. Once the engine has been designed, built, tested, and accepted, this company will produce these engines for ACME's upgraded product.

The motor company uses two major types of information asset from ACME. The first type consists of engineering plans, specifications, technical descriptions, and so on for the motor; these are mostly stored and processed in the company's computer-aided design and manufacturing application. The other type of information asset is business-focused and includes data such as the price per unit ACME pays the company and the projected number of units ACME is ordering for the next few quarters.

Disclosing the engineering plans for the new motor to a competitor would have a significant financial impact on ACME, perhaps greater than the money spent to develop the engine because of the potential impact to ACME's competitiveness. On the other hand, although disclosure of unit cost and production rates to a competitor is undesirable, it doesn't cause as much damage. Thus the corresponding value of such information is less than that of the engine design. One other interesting question to ask when considering the value of the engine design is, What would it cost ACME if someone were able to change the design in an inconspicuous way before production so that all of the motors produced were defective and the products including them had to be recalled?

After the identification phase is completed, the security team members meet to organize and compare their findings. They create an information asset table that includes a row for each identified information asset. At this point, the table has two columns next to an information asset's name. The first is an indication of its value and the second is the primary department responsible for the information asset. At this point, ACME uses only three value levels: critical, important, and minor. The security team decides to store the information asset table in a database in the IT department. This phase of the process finishes with a short presentation to the CEO and his staff that highlights ACME's critical information assets. The next step is to determine just how well ACME currently protects these assets.

Determining Your Current Vulnerabilities

Once you've identified your company's information assets, the next step is to determine who is able to get to them. You can then compare who *can* access an asset with who *should* be able to access it. The number of people, or types of people, who shouldn't be able to but can get to a company's information is one measure of the risk to these assets.

The task of figuring out who can get to an information asset requires two perspectives. The first is determining who can access an information asset because a company's current security protections allow him to. The second perspective involves assuming the role of a hacker and determining all of the subversive methods that could be used to raid information assets. A company needs to look at both perspectives to gain a full picture of its current vulnerabilities.

LEGITIMATE ACCESS TO INFORMATION

A company's sensitive information can be at risk even if no one tries to breach its security mechanisms. This occurs when the security mechanisms a company uses don't offer the protection the company wants or expects. There are many reasons why this can happen: The security technology a company needs didn't exist at the time it purchased a security solution; the company doesn't have a well-thought-out policy concerning access to its information assets; or the employee setting up the security protections for an information asset doesn't know what the policy is.

The process of determining who is allowed to access an information asset is a direct continuation of the asset identification process of chapter 1 and focuses on the software that manages information assets. Most software applications include security functions to enforce who can and can't access the information. For example, a customer relationship management application controls who can see and change data about specific customers. The employees who administer these applications can describe what access to information assets is currently permitted as well as the choices a company has for making changes in the application's access permissions.

Companies can usually find application administrators within their IT function. Depending on a company's size, that function may range from a large dedicated department, augmented by IT staff assigned to other departments, to a single, part-time employee. The second place to look for administrators is within individual company departments. An engineering or marketing communications group might set up its own internal Web site to share information on a particular project, and the person who set up the site would be the administrator.

The information an administrator can provide can take several forms. It might be a list of names of people who have permission to access a particular asset, or a list of groups of people or even a list of other computers that have access to certain software applications. Options for changing access permissions might include granting new permissions or revoking current permissions that a user has to a particular asset. For example, permission to read a weekly sales status report could be taken away from an employee if he changes job functions.

Once a company knows who—or what—is currently permitted to access its information assets and the range of options it has for changing these permissions, it can decide if it should make any changes. One reason for changing permissions is to close security holes—for instance, if it's discovered that some employees who shouldn't be allowed to can see a company's quarterly financial results before they are published. Another reason is to provide greater access if a company's current access permissions are preventing employees from getting the information they need to do their jobs efficiently or to pursue new business opportunities.

Changing the permissions users have within a company's current information security solution is one example of how the corporate security process addresses company security needs as quickly as possible, but in the context of a comprehensive effort. By taking short-term actions with a long-term view, companies can make simple fixes without having to wait until they finish the process to benefit.

USING THE INFORMATION ASSET TABLE

During the corporate security process, a company needs to gather, analyze, and act on a significant amount of information about its assets. After the completion of the security process, companies still need to use and update this information to keep their solutions in sync with evolving business requirements and security technology. The information asset table provides a single, logical place to maintain this data. There are two criteria for determining what goes into the table: if the data will help a company protect its information assets, and if the data will help a company know how its information is currently protected and can be protected in the future.

Chapter 1 introduced the first three fields that go into the information asset table: the name of the asset, its value, and the department or group responsible for the asset. This chapter introduces three more relevant details about an information asset (see table 2-1). The first is the application that manages and provides security protection for an asset. The second is the current permissions the application allows for access to an asset, and the third is a description of all of the available permissions the application could allow for an asset. The first two fields provide information on how an information asset is currently protected, while the third field provides information that helps determine how an information asset may be protected in the future. (See table 1-1 for a description of all the components of a complete information asset table.)

The first entry in the information asset table is the term sheet for a proposed corporate acquisition. In order to access the term sheet, it's necessary to use the executive staff's internal Web site, and the Web site controls who can access it. The current permissions allow each member of the executive staff to read and update the term sheet. The available permissions show that the executives could also be given permission to delete the term sheet. In the second table entry, an enterprise application controls permissions for the customer record, permitting the customer's sales rep to read and update the record, while only allowing a sales manager to read the record.

TABLE 2-1

Information Asset Table: Application and Permissions

Asset Name	Application	Current Permissions	Available Permissions
Term sheet for a corporate acquisition	Internal Web site for executive management	Each executive can read and update term sheet	Read, update, and delete term sheet
Customer record	Customer relationship management (CRM) software	Sales rep can read and update record; sales manager can read report	Read, update, and delete record
Company phone book	HR database	HR department can create, read, update, and delete employee records	Create, read, update, and delete record

It's not necessary or desirable to put every single bit of data about information assets into the table. It's often better just to indicate where the data can be found. When a business manager is reviewing the protections for an asset, it doesn't matter where the answer is, only that he can find it easily. For example, an entry in the Current Permissions field could reference access control information within the application managing the information asset in question. Likewise, an entry in the Available Permissions field could reference an online copy of the application's administrative manual. Minimizing the amount of data that is actually stored within the table greatly reduces the effort required to keep the table up to date. For example, it won't be necessary to update the table whenever the permissions on an information asset change.

If the prospect of finding and recording the necessary data on a company's information assets still seems overwhelming, you can begin with groups of information assets instead of individual assets. Examples of asset groups are all of the assets managed by an enterprise application, all of the assets available through a group's Web site, and all of the assets on a specific computer. Once a company gets its arms around its information assets at this high level, it can drill down to the individual assets in each of these groups, according to time, budget, and priority. The information asset table performs the function of a bookmark so companies won't lose their place.

SUBVERSIVE ACCESS TO INFORMATION

To understand subversive ways of accessing corporate information, you need to work like a hacker. There are many definitions for the term *hacker*, ranging from an experienced computer programmer to a vandal or criminal. In this book, a hacker is someone who tries to get unauthorized access to a company's computers, networks, and information assets. The tools—which are legal—and techniques that companies use to determine their vulnerability to this kind of attack are in many cases the same ones hackers use.

The first step is to find out how much information a hacker any-where in the world can discover about your company's computers and the software that runs on them. To do this, a company would use a tool called a port scanner that finds all of its computers that can be reached from the Internet, and the software that runs on each. This software includes popular enterprise applications as well as services such as e-mail and Web browsing, plus the operating systems (e.g., Windows or UNIX) that manage the computers themselves. Many port scanning products can produce maps of the computer network they scan, thus enabling a hacker to visualize his target better.

All programs have "bugs," or programming errors, some of which hackers can exploit to take control over a computer. The next steps a hacker would take would be to find out if any of the programs running on your company's computers have security bugs and then exploit them. Companies can look to software and hardware vendors, infor-mation security organizations, and underground hacker Web sites to find this information. On hacker Web sites, companies can also find carefully crafted programs that will take advantage of security bugs in a program and cause it to misbehave in a way that allows the hacker to take control of the computer and all of its assets. "Scripts" and "ex-ploits" are two names hackers use for these programs, and no skill is required to use them.

Protecting companies against this common form of attack is a straightforward process. Companies should install, as quickly as pos-sible, the security updates that software vendors distribute to fix these security vulnerabilities, and this should become a routine part of a company's IT operations. Unfortunately, hackers are able to exploit se-curity bugs long after the fixes become available, in part because of corporate priorities for IT departments. Revenue or productivity-generating activities, such as maintaining an e-commerce Web site or setting up computers for employees, often take precedence over in-stalling security updates.

In addition to breaking into company computers, hackers can ac-cess corporate information assets by intercepting them while they are traveling over computer networks, such as the Internet or a company's own internal network. The difficulty of this task varies according to the type of network, with fiber-optic networks being the most difficult to tap and wireless networks the easiest. Intercepting information on a wireless network is easy because there's no wire to tap; all of the information is in the air, easy prey for a hacker with a wireless laptop. To get the information a hacker wants, he'll use another tool called a network sniffer. Sniffers capture the messages that travel over a network and translate them into a form that people can understand. It takes very little instruction to train someone to use a network sniffer and listen in to all of the information on a wireless network. Many corporate IT departments already use network sniffers to diagnose performance problems on their networks.

ACME REVIEWS ITS SECURITY SITUATION

At this point, ACME is ready to look at some of the legitimate and subversive means of accessing its information assets. The security team decides to start with its product management group. Product managers' responsibilities include translating customer requests and needs into product and feature requirements for the R&D department. Each product manager has a laptop that connects directly into ACME's internal network when a product manager is in the office. When out of the office, a product manager can use a modem to dial into the company network.

First, ACME looks at an internal Web site that its product managers use for the development of white papers and marketing requirements documents. The Web site contains drafts and final versions of the documents as well as materials such as industry analyst reports, in-depth analyses of competitors and their products, and ACME strategic plans. In order to access these information assets, product managers type the Web site address into their browsers. The security team realizes that this means that anyone who is connected to ACME's internal network can access these assets if they know the Web site address.

Next, ACME studies an internal order entry application that product managers use for sending products to business partners free of charge. Partner companies use these complementary products when they develop, test, and market products of their own that interoperate with ACME's products. Product managers log on to this application, which was developed in-house, by entering a username and password to ensure that only authorized users (employees) are able to place orders. However, there are no additional security checks to limit which products a particular product manager can order or the number of products she can order.

The third area the security team examines is how the IT department services employees' laptops. They discover that all of ACME's computers are configured to allow IT administrators to remotely control them. This helps administrators understand and fix problems much more efficiently than would be the case if they had to go to each employee's office. It also means that IT administrators can access information on computers belonging to any ACME employee.

To understand subversive routes to information, the security team decides to mount an attack on information assets in a remote sales office. Using a port scanner, they learn the names of most of the software running on the computers and compare what they find against a list of exploits on a hacker Web site. They find an exploit for the Web server software that's on one of the computers in that office and use it to take over the computer. Then they create a new user account with complete administrative permissions on that computer.

After completing this phase of the corporate security process, the security team meets with senior management to discuss their discoveries and prioritize the next steps. The VP of marketing says he wants to limit access to the product managers' Web site to employees of the marketing department, but he doesn't want to spend any additional money on security. The security team responds by instructing an IT administrator to password-protect the Web site and give the password to the VP's administrative assistant for distribution throughout the marketing department, with instructions not to share the password with anyone outside of the department. The security team makes it clear that this is not an ideal solution, but will provide a greater degree of protection than currently exists without spending any money. There is little concern at this meeting over the lack of controls once a product manager logs on to the order entry system, because there are enough external controls, such as the shipping department's strict attention to anything unusual, to be able to spot any fraud. But there is significant concern among the executives that anyone in the IT department can view all of the information on their laptops. They were not aware that IT staff could do this, and so they raise fixing this to a high priority.

The security team had been getting some resistance from the sales department, who view participation in the security process as a waste of time, compared with time spent on customers. So during this meeting, the security team explains how they broke into the sales computer and logged on to the computer using their new account. They then demonstrate how they could read and delete all of the information on that computer. The exercise works: The sales department realizes that security breaches could affect their ability to close sales and thus their commissions. The security team then recommends and the executive team approves allocating money to the IT department to install security patches regularly.

THREE

Protecting Your Computers

At this point many businesspeople might think their information security work is done. They know what information assets they have and who can get to them, and they've installed security updates to foil hackers. They may even have virus protection and firewalls thrown in for good measure. What more is there to do? Lots.

Technologies like firewalls and antivirus software protect computers, but they don't provide adequate protection for a company's information assets or its business operations. Ask yourself two questions:

- For each information asset and automated business process your company has, ask, What security technologies protect it?

- For each security technology, ask, Which information assets and automated business processes does this protect?

If you can't answer the first question, then there is no reason to believe your company is protected. If you can't answer the second question, then there is no reason to believe that your company is spending its information security budget wisely. Many companies spend most of their IT security budget on technologies and practices that protect computers, but do not directly protect any information asset. Security measures such as port scans, security patches, virus protection, and firewalls are important, but only as a subset of a larger security process.

Companies tend to focus primarily on computer-based security for two main reasons: media attention and simplicity. The public exposure that comes from news articles about crashed Web sites, stolen credit card numbers, and virus attacks puts great pressure on companies to act. And deploying virus protection software, erecting firewalls, and installing security updates are all largely independent, straightforward tasks that work well as individual budget line items and can be "checked off" once they're completed.

The problem with focusing on computer security is that it can't completely answer the prior questions about protecting sensitive company information. This leaves companies with lingering doubt about just how well protected they and their information are. It's important to understand how these technologies work and what protections they can and can't provide.

FIREWALLS: A PERIMETER DEFENSE

Firewalls—a combination of hardware and/or software that stands between computers and the Internet—get a lot of attention, and deservedly so. The number of computers connected to the Internet is still increasing dramatically, from roughly 97 million in 2000 to more than 137 million in 2001, and each one is a potential security threat.[1] To attack a computer that is not connected to the Internet, a hacker has to be physically next to the computer or know the phone number to dial a modem, if the computer has one. With the Internet, an attacker doesn't have either of these constraints. All he needs is a name—for example, www.company.com—that identifies a company computer, and he can use the port scanning vulnerability tools described in chapter 2 to find and exploit a security hole.

One of the lessons from chapter 2 is that a hacker needs to exploit only one vulnerability in a computer to take it over. Even if a company routinely installs all security patches as soon as they become available, its assets are still not safe because a computer can have security vulnerabilities for which security patches have not yet been distributed. Multiplying the security problems of a single computer by the number of computers within a company shows the need for a better approach to protecting computers from Internet-based attacks.

Firewalls are a perimeter defense, like fences or moats. The reason for using a firewall is to turn a very difficult security problem into a more manageable one. Instead of each computer having total responsibility for protecting itself, the firewall becomes the first line of defense for all of them.

Part of the appeal of a perimeter defense is simplicity. It is a strategy that is easy to understand, and it is less expensive to erect and maintain a perimeter defense around a company's internal network of computers than it is to fortify each computer within the company to the same degree. A perimeter defense also creates an environment in which day-to-day company activities, such as group collaboration via an internal Web site, can take place without threat from the outside world. Since the perimeter defense is responsible for protection against Internet-based attacks, the protection of individual computers needs to address only the threats from within the company's internal network. Likewise, the cost of protecting an individual computer can be balanced against the value of the information assets stored on the computer. Within a pharmaceutical company, for example, a computer containing information about a drug under development probably warrants more protection than a computer containing marketing literature.

How Firewalls Work

The goal of any perimeter defense system is to limit interaction between the outside world and the inside world to a small number of well-guarded gates. Given the presence of the word "wall" in firewall, it is easy to think a firewall is the same thing as a city wall. But a firewall is actually the equivalent of a gate. It controls the information that passes between a company's computers and the Internet.

A firewall can take a number of approaches to control interaction with the Internet. A firewall can enforce a policy that only specific computers on the Internet can communicate with specific company computers.[2] Other firewalls permit communication from a computer on the Internet to a company computer only if the company computer first contacted the Internet computer.[3] Still other firewalls examine the messages passing through the perimeter and permit only traffic of a specific kind, such as Web browsing or database access, to pass to a specific company computer.[4]

A firewall can adopt one of two basic policies to control access from the Internet to an internal computer. The first is "whatever is not prohibited is allowed," and the second is "whatever is not allowed is prohibited." The first policy is similar to having a rule at a city gate that allows everyone to pass except those whose names are on a list of known criminals. The second policy allows people to pass only if their names are on a list of approved visitors. This second policy is more secure, but it can be annoying if a firewall has not been configured to support all the types of Internet communication that are required for business. For example, some companies configure their firewalls to prevent employees from downloading large files from the Internet, which is a real problem for employees who are conducting research during the development of a new product.

If a firewall functions like a gate, a reasonable question to ask is, What functions like a wall? Within a computing environment, nothing actually functions as a wall, except the absence of a connection to the Internet. While an invading army can travel over land, sea, or air to attack a city, a hacker can use the Internet only to attack a computer that is connected to the Internet. In order for a firewall to be effective in protecting company computers, it has to be the only connection these computers have to the Internet. In a large company with many computers, the task of ensuring that every Internet connection goes through a firewall can be quite difficult. For example, many hardware vendors include dial-up modems in the computers they sell to companies, which lets service people easily connect to the computers to perform maintenance and fix problems. And many companies have computers that ordinarily connect to the Internet through the corporate firewall but still have working modems no one is aware of. These individual connections from company computers to computers on the Internet that don't go through a firewall are called backside connections and pose a significant risk to companies.

What Firewalls Can't Do

The primary security protection firewalls provide, as figure 3-1A shows, is blocking attacks from the Internet, such as the hacker exploits described in chapter 2.

But what can't they do? The answers are the same as for any type of perimeter defense. A firewall offers no protection against security attacks that don't cross the perimeter, such as those that originate within an organization (figure 3-1B). A firewall will not protect a company from an employee in customer service who makes fraudulent purchases using a customer's credit card number, for example. Nor will a firewall protect against Internet attacks that misuse approved paths,

FIGURE 3-1

The Limits of Firewall Protection

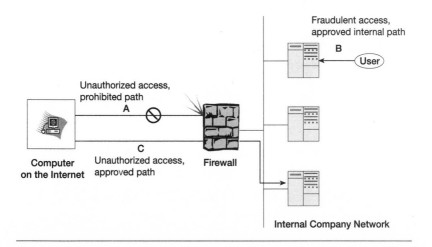

such as those for accessing databases, as shown in figure 3-1C. A firewall can't stop someone from trying to get company information he's not authorized to see because it can't tell the difference between a valid request for information and attempted theft.

VIRUS PROTECTION: AN ENDLESS BATTLE

Viruses are probably the most visible information security problem computer users experience personally. Spreading quickly and quietly, they can cripple a company's e-mail system, corrupt or delete important computer files, or halt worker productivity until they're eliminated. Eliminating a virus can be frustrating and time-consuming because a virus can quickly reinfect a company's computers if all traces of it are not removed. Viruses such as the infamous one dubbed "I Love You" propagate across the Internet as e-mail attachments. The message in the e-mail carrying the virus instructs the recipient to open the attachment, which launches the virus. The virus then damages numerous files on the recipient's computer and e-mails itself to everyone in the recipient's address book.

One of the lessons learned from such virus infections is to never open a suspicious e-mail attachment, even if it comes from someone you know. While sound advice, this vigilance doesn't ensure complete protection.

Consider, for example, opening a word processing file that a colleague sends as an e-mail attachment. It appears to be a safe situation because you are expecting the file, and since it's just a report and not a program, you assume it can't do any harm. But what happens when you open the document and a macro inside the report starts to run? Macros are computer programs that perform a wide variety of tasks, from formatting paragraphs to sending e-mail and visiting Web sites. But they can also contain viruses that can do as much damage to your computer and its information as other viruses can. In this common business scenario, there is nothing about the e-mail or attachment to raise anyone's suspicion.

The only solution available to companies and individuals is to use a virus protection program that can check for the presence of viruses the moment they arrive at a computer and before they have a chance to do any harm. At a minimum, a virus protection program should detect and protect against viruses that arrive via e-mail, from Web sites, or may already exist on a computer.

How Virus Protection Works

Virus protection programs work by scanning files for recognizable virus characteristics, also known as virus definitions or virus signatures. A virus protection program compares a suspected file against its collection of virus definitions, looking for a match. For instance, it looks for viruses that have the characteristics of the notorious "Melissa" or "Code Red" viruses that plagued the Internet several years ago. If there is a match, the virus protection program can continue with a number of options, such as trying to remove the virus from the file, deleting the file, or quarantining the file.

One shortcoming of this approach is that a virus protection program can only protect against viruses it already knows about. (Virus protection vendors are developing more sophisticated ways of recognizing new viruses, but it remains true that they can't detect a virus if they don't know what they're looking for.) This causes two crucial delays: first, the time it takes for a virus protection vendor to write a new definition to recognize the virus; and second, the time it takes for companies to load the new definition into the virus protection programs running on their computers. In general, vendors respond quickly to new viruses, so the first time delay poses a limited risk to companies. In practice, the second time delay poses a much greater threat.

Why Virus Protection Falls Short

For companies, the biggest decision is whether to centralize virus detection and virus definition updates or distribute the responsibility. In the centralized approach, virus protection programs run on the computers that send and receive e-mail for the company and on computers that process Web site requests. One benefit of the centralized model is that responsibility for installing and configuring virus protection programs and ensuring that definitions are up to date is in the hands of administrators who are trained for and assigned to these tasks, as opposed to individual users who may not perform these tasks correctly, or at all. One drawback to this approach is that individual company computers are not protected from viruses that enter a computer through some path other than the corporate e-mail server or that may already be on a computer. For instance, many employees have e-mail accounts that they maintain for personal use and access from their company-owned computer.

Virus protection vendors have tried to remedy this situation by offering enterprise versions of their products that allow IT administrators to install virus protection programs on all company computers, including laptops, and to configure virus definition updates to take place frequently without action by individual employees.

However, companies are still at risk if they do not configure and use these virus protection programs correctly. One *Fortune* 500 company I consulted with deployed an enterprise virus protection program on every company computer. The IT department configured the program to automatically check corporate e-mail for viruses and to get virus definition updates every day. But the company didn't configure the program to check nonwork e-mail accounts or programs downloaded from the Internet for viruses. It would have been easy for employees to enable these protections by marking two checkboxes on the virus protection program on their computers, but they didn't know they needed to because the company told employees that the new virus protection program worked automatically. The problem wasn't the result of any security shortcoming in the virus protection program. It was the fault of the company, which configured its virus protection program without considering all of the sources of risk that arise from the ways employees use company computers.

INTRUSION DETECTION AND MANAGED SECURITY SERVICES

Intrusion detection and security monitoring is an increasingly popular approach to protecting corporate computers and internal networks. The motivation is the recognition that it's impossible to prevent all attacks, and therefore it's good to know when an attack is under way so there is an opportunity to stop it before it does harm. In order to detect attacks, a company places monitors throughout its internal network to collect information on computer and network usage that might indicate an attack. An intrusion detection program analyzes this information and notifies an IT employee in the event that further analysis or action is needed. Some intrusion detection programs use attack signatures, which are comparable to virus definitions, to identify potential trouble. This provides a useful backup in the event that an attack makes it through a firewall or other computer security measures fail.

One problem with intrusion detection programs is that they can only catch actions that they believe are attacks, which means they are playing the same catch-up game that virus protection plays. However, the more significant problem is that they don't protect against people who abuse their legitimate right to company information. For example, if an employee in the accounts payable department creates and pays invoices as a part of her job, an intrusion detection system won't know if she creates and pays a fraudulent invoice and pockets the money. Nor will it be able to detect a hacker doing the same thing, if the hacker logged on to a computer as that employee.

Some companies choose to outsource the ongoing tasks related to protecting their computers and networks. Companies that do this sort of work are called managed security services firms. Their offerings can include

- routine port scanning for vulnerabilities,

- installation of security patches and upgrades,

- firewall management,

- virus protection management, and

- intrusion detection monitoring.

These companies have staff on duty twenty-four hours a day to address emergencies. They can sort through all of a company's security reports and alerts so that company IT employees don't have to and can help companies prepare for and respond to attacks. They commonly have one or more secure operations centers that connect to client company computers over the Internet. These network connections retrieve information from the monitors placed on client computers and networks that could indicate intrusions or attacks. Managed security services firms can also use network connections to change how a firewall works, install security updates, or fend off a hacker.

Many companies find managed security services an attractive solution, but giving away so much control over company computers to an outside firm poses a huge potential risk. A firm that provides the services just listed has complete control over a company's computers and so has the capability to disclose, corrupt, and destroy all of a company's information assets. Before engaging a managed security services firm, a company needs to understand what the firm does to protect a company's information assets and business operations from the potential threats the firm itself poses.

Here are a few examples of questions a company should ask as part of its due diligence: What prevents a hacker from impersonating a secure operations center and attacking company computers? What prevents a rogue employee at the managed security firm from destroying company information instead of installing security patches? Since a secure operations center supports many different clients, what prevents the leaking of sensitive information relating to one client to another or prevents one client from using its connection to a secure operations center to attack another client? What records does the firm keep on its employees' actions so they can be held accountable for what they've done?

All of these questions focus on how a company performs its business services in a way that doesn't harm a client's information assets. And none of these questions can be answered by the firm saying it has firewalls or virus protection or any of the other security services it offers because none of these services speaks directly to the use and protection of a client's information assets. In order for one company to do business with another company—whether a security firm or any type of business—they both need to understand how their information assets and business operations are protected in the course of the business relationship. And that's where the Trust Framework comes into play.

FOUR

Developing a Security Process Based on Trust

What role does trust play in information security? Before diving into that weighty question, it's important to remember a few key points. First, the corporate security process is not about protecting a company's *computers,* but about protecting a *company* and its information assets. Second, while there are plenty of technical measures a company can take to reduce the vulnerability of its computers to attack (as discussed in chapter 3), these measures aren't complete and don't comprehensively address a company's information security needs. This chapter describes the Trust Framework, a unique way of thinking about information security that enables a company to move from a defensive stance, always reacting to the next attack, to a proactive position of strength.

To understand how the Trust Framework can help, first consider the case of an enterprising entrepreneur who wants to start a biotechnology company, but doesn't want to spend years and millions of dollars on research and development to create a new drug. How would he go about this? The answer is simple: Steal other companies' intellectual property.

Initially, he considers hacking into the computer systems of his major competitors, but decides that's too time-consuming. Instead, he focuses on a law firm that specializes in biotechnology patents. By their very nature, patent applications deal with significant innovation, and they must be written so that someone in the field will be able to understand and build the invention. Since the law firm he selects represents a number of biotech companies, he will have access to a wide variety of high-quality information, all with the convenience of one-stop shopping.

The first phase of his plan is to get a username and password that will let him into the law firm's computers without causing suspicion. His goal is to find the password for someone in the IT department who has an administrative account, but even a regular user account will do as a step on the way to administrative powers. He begins this task by using social engineering, a technical term in the security field for lying. A typical ruse is to call an employee and pose as a computer operator who needs a user's password in order to perform some official task, or to pose as a harried fellow employee who needs a password to finish a critical project.

If that fails, he can continue his search for passwords by dumpster diving, or "trashint" in the jargon of professional corporate spies. He'll look through the firm's trash for Post-Its or scraps of paper containing usernames and passwords, or for computer documentation that indicates which operating systems, such as Windows 2000 or Solaris, run on the firm's computers. This can be a great tactic, since companies often never change the default administrative passwords on the software they buy. Once he has an administrative account's password, the next step is finding the information he is looking for.

Instead of searching through all of the files on the firm's computers, he focuses on the computer that handles and routes all of the firm's e-mail. He installs a program that scans all of the law firm's e-mails as they travel through this computer and sends copies of the ones he's interested in to an e-mail account he created for this purpose. The program filters the e-mail messages according to a set of criteria he specifies—for example, e-mails in which the "To" or "From" address fields match biotechnology competitors he's targeting. He could also have the program look for keywords in the "Subject" line, in the body of the e-mail, or in attachments to narrow his search. This would be helpful if he were interested only in gene sequencing, for instance.

In the event that his program is discovered and someone realizes what he's done, he doesn't want any connection between him and the forwarded e-mails. So he uses a free e-mail account, such as Yahoo! or Hotmail, and checks this e-mail only from a public computer, such as one in a cyber café, copy center, or library, that is not too close to his home or work so he won't be recognized.

That's all he needs to do in order to have a stream of state-of-the-art biotech secrets sent to him with the convenience of a clipping service. But what's to stop him from doing more? He could decide to start patenting another company's invention. A significant number of exchanges between an inventor and a patent attorney take place while a patent application is being drafted. When he notices these exchanges starting, he can move quickly to file his own patent application before they do and thus rob them of the revenue and competitive advantage the patent would have afforded.

The techniques described above have all been used in real life, if not for this specific purpose. The purpose of this example is not to alarm, but to show that security measures such as firewalls, virus protection, and security updates don't protect against this type of attack.

The Trust Framework can. The Trust Framework provides companies with a straightforward process for understanding how to protect themselves and their information assets so they can achieve their business objectives. It does this by helping businesses determine the information security solutions they need for their business activities.

THE TRUST FRAMEWORK DEFINED

Consider a company that wants to reduce expenses by providing customer self-service over the Internet. In addition to basic business concerns such as budgeting and staffing, the company must think seriously about the security implications of its decision. It must find and purchase the security technologies it needs in order to make the Internet transactions safe.

Using the Trust Framework, the company begins by identifying the trust objectives for this new business activity. In this case, the objectives are the same online as they are offline. Offline, customer service representatives need to know that a person requesting a change to an account is the customer in question; that the changes made to an account (e.g., reversing a charge) are done in accordance with company policy; that customer information is kept private; and that disputes can be settled by reviewing records of customer requests and customer service representative actions. It's important for the company to explicitly list its trust objectives, so it can understand how the shift to handling these transactions online changes the security implications. The customer service example just mentioned illustrates the four general types of trust objectives. These relate more specifically to identity, access, confidentiality, and authenticity.

With these clearly articulated trust objectives, the company then selects the information security technologies and procedures that will meet these objectives. These security measures, or trust evidence, include requiring that users enter unique usernames and passwords to authenticate themselves to the customer service application before making any changes to their accounts. Other evidence includes the use of encryption to keep all the information private; strict access control for the company employees charged with taking care of requests, such as refunds, that the application can't handle automatically; and the ability to record all employee and customer activity on the Internet transaction system. Some of this evidence corresponds directly to protective measures the company used in the past. For example, logging on to the application serves the same function as telling a customer service representative an account number and the last four digits of a Social Security number. Similarly, an electronic record of Internet transactions serves the same purpose as voice recordings of customer service calls. But other trust evidence—for example, encrypting customer communications—wasn't necessary offline because telephone conversations are more difficult to intercept.

In short, *the Trust Framework is a two-step process for companies to select the information security technology they need:*

1. Identify the trust objectives appropriate for the company's business transactions and uses of its information assets.

2. Select information security technologies based on their capacity to satisfy these trust objectives.

You may wonder why an approach used to select security technology is called a Trust Framework. The reason is that trust, and not security, is a more important concept to understand if you want to protect your company. The *American Heritage Dictionary* defines *secure* as "free from danger or attack," and many people think of information security in these absolute terms.[1] Something either is secure or it isn't, they reason, and secure means secure today, tomorrow, next year, under all circumstances, and against all current or future attacks. But that is dangerous and incorrect thinking. In fact, the answer to the question, "Is my computer system secure?" will always be no. There is no amount of money a company can spend to make its computer systems completely free from danger or attack, and it is a waste of corporate resources to have this abstract goal.

Instead, companies should focus on understanding the types and degrees of protection they need, given their specific circumstances. This is where trust enters the discussion. Unlike the black-and-white definition of secure, there are different degrees of trust. In general, people have greater trust in the more familiar than they do in the less familiar. For example, a businessperson will have greater trust in a colleague with whom he works every day than in someone he met a few times at business meetings. These different degrees of trust directly affect how a businessperson acts when working with different people. In particular, the level of trust affects the subjects the businessperson will address, his degree of candor, and the types of activities he's willing to collaborate on. The greater the trust, the more productive the business collaboration.

Similarly, people require a higher degree of trust in some situations than they do in others. For example, a person requires a much higher degree of trust in the qualifications and ability of a surgeon who is about to perform a triple bypass operation on him than he does in the person who is about to wash his car. This means that it takes different types and amounts of evidence to establish the degree of trust needed. The evidence a patient requires may include multiple references from physicians he knows, board certification, and statistics on number of operations performed and patient results. In contrast, employment at a car wash may be ample evidence for someone to trust a person to wash his car.

These two examples demonstrate another element of trust, which is that the emphasis is on who is doing the trusting and what they need in order to establish their trust. Consider ACME's interest in starting a partnership that entails sharing sensitive information with another company. The latter company may assert that its computers are secure and that ACME's information will be safe, but to take that company at its word is foolish business practice, akin to believing the claims of a used car salesman. Rather, ACME needs to gather enough evidence to assure itself that its information will be protected while in the other company's care. Some of this evidence may very well come from the other company, but the process is complete only when ACME has achieved the necessary confidence.

Another aspect of trust that bears on business decision making is that the amount of evidence it takes to establish similar degrees of trust can vary significantly from one company and situation to another. Two military organizations I consulted with provide an example of how this works in real life. Both organizations needed a very high degree of confidence that the people using their computers were who they said they were. To establish this high level of trust in user identities, one organization used security technology that required users to enter three passwords, one of which was generated by a small cryptographic device, before they could log on. The other organization, with an even more urgent need to know who was using their computers, didn't even require users to log on at all. Why?

In this particular case, to enter one of the rooms where a computer was located, a person had to pass through numerous armed checkpoints where his identity was verified, in some cases by guards who had known him personally for years. Having passed through the checkpoints, he was the only person allowed in the computer room during his shift. In this situation, requiring three passwords and a cryptographic token wasn't sufficient to establish trust in a user's identity, whereas the low-tech approach of checkpoints and personal recognition was.

One lesson from these military examples is that it is much more important to focus on the protection a business needs rather than the security features a computer has. A second lesson is that businesses need to consider their entire operational environments when deciding on the security technologies they need to meet their trust objectives. By taking this broader perspective, businesses not only help ensure the effectiveness of the security technologies they purchase, but may also discover that expensive security technology is not always what they need.

FOUR IMPORTANT TRUST OBJECTIVES

The Trust Framework organizes trust objectives into four areas:

1. confidentiality,

2. identity,

3. access, and

4. authenticity.

Categorizing trust objectives this way helps a company determine its information security requirements. Without such a structure, it is difficult to know where to begin or when the process is finished. In addition, these four trust objectives correspond closely to different types of information security products and services. This grouping thus simplifies the process of selecting and purchasing security solutions.

Confidentiality covers objectives related to keeping sensitive business information secret. Identity covers objectives related to knowing and verifying the identities of all people and companies with whom one has online business dealings. Access addresses objectives centered on making sure that only authorized people and companies have access to the business information and resources they need. Authenticity addresses the objectives of having believable business information as well as indisputable records of business transactions and human actions.

Confidentiality

Confidentiality is both a requirement and an expectation for any communication or information exchange relating to sensitive business activities, such as contract negotiations. Conversations between negotiators that take place in private are presumed to be secret, as are written proposals and negotiation positions that in a non-digital world might be locked in offices and file cabinets. These confidentiality protections help establish the trust necessary for all parties to negotiate in good faith. In a non-digital scenario, someone would need to physically take a proposal from a locked office to violate that confidentiality.

As business records are increasingly stored on computers and communication more frequently takes place over the Internet, the protections that businesses have relied on in the non-digital world start to disappear and must be replaced with new protections. Since it's no longer possible to physically protect information from an attacker, the answer is to render the information useless to an attacker. Encryption, which has been used for more than two thousand years, is the technology of choice for accomplishing this task.

Identity

When a customer enters a bank for the first time to open an account, she can use numerous pieces of evidence to establish that she is in a bank and her money will be safe. These include signage, an FDIC notice, and the presence of tellers, guards, and other customers. Likewise, the bank can use various pieces of evidence, such as a driver's license or credit card, to establish the identity of the new customer. The evidence that each uses to verify the other's identity is familiar.

One reason why reliably establishing identity in the digital world is so difficult is that familiar evidence doesn't exist. Most of the attributes that are important to know about a person or business online originate in the real world. The challenge is to understand what it takes to trust that a digital identity corresponds to the real-world person or business you think it does. This involves both corporate and individual procedures as well as technologies such as passwords, encryption, and digital certificates.

Access

Establishing the identity of a business partner isn't an end in itself. It is useful only if it helps a company decide what kind of interaction it will have with that business partner and what information the company will share with it. For example, a company will share product engineering diagrams with a supplier that is manufacturing a part for the product. And it will share customer and sales information with a company that acts as a sales channel. But it probably won't share product engineering diagrams with its sales partner, nor will it share detailed sales information with a supplier.

Within a computer system, a business can control access to information assets and the applications that use these assets. Every business activity that can be performed using a computer entails access to information assets and applications, so controlling computer-enabled business activities comes down to controlling access. This is true whether the activity is purchasing stock over the Internet or collaborating on the score for a new movie. The purpose of an access control system is to enable a company to put information into the hands of those who need it while keeping it from those who shouldn't have it. Companies should select security technology based on the types of access policies they want to enforce.

Authenticity

The final trust objective relates to knowing what's real in the digital world. One of the fundamental differences between the physical and digital worlds is the ease with which digital information can be changed without a trace. When a company purchases supplies, it wants a receipt so it has recourse in the event that the supplier claims the company didn't pay. Similarly, a brokerage firm wants a reliable record of its clients' trading instructions and its brokers' actions, in case a question or dispute arises later on. Access controls can't prevent a broker from misusing his legitimate permissions or a customer from lying, which is why a reliable record is so important. The kind of information a company needs to record and the lengths it will go to protect it vary significantly from one business situation to another. Companies can use technologies such as audit trails and digital signatures to ensure authenticity.

In chapters 5, 6, 7, and 8, you'll learn about these four trust objectives in more detail, and how information security technologies can provide the trust evidence to meet your business objectives.

FIVE

Keeping Information Confidential

In the summer of 2001, Avi Rubin, a security expert from AT&T Laboratories in Florham Park, New Jersey, brought his laptop with him to a nearby hospital so he could do some work while waiting for his wife to recover from minor surgery.[1] He noticed that the hospital's wireless network was configured to allow full access to any other wireless computer in the hospital, including his. This meant that he was able to tap into a high-speed connection to the Internet from the waiting room. It also meant that if he turned on the network sniffer program he had on his laptop, he could see every message traveling throughout the hospital, from sensitive patient information that nurses entered on the wireless-equipped laptops they carried from room to room to billing and insurance information.

Rubin did not, in fact, view any patient information, but instead wrote a letter to hospital administrators to inform them of the vulnerability. They responded that he had found only a temporary security problem that was the result of a computer upgrade. This explanation would not provide much consolation if someone's medical records were disclosed or modified during this "upgrade process."

The first trust objective in the Trust Framework is the confidentiality or secrecy of a company's information assets. This addresses the need to prevent prying eyes from seeing, and in some cases changing, sensitive corporate information and the resulting damage to business activities. The value of a company's shampoo formula would drop significantly if a competitor knew it and could produce a less expensive, equivalent product. The disclosure of company information could also prevent it from successfully executing business plans. For example, a competitor who knows the details of a company's negotiations with a potential exclusive distributor could use that information to finalize a preemptive contract with the same distributor.

In today's business environment, encryption provides the trust evidence businesses need to meet the trust objective of maintaining confidentiality of corporate information. Encryption works in situations where other security technologies can't provide adequate protection, such as when information is traveling over networks between computers, or when information is stored on a computer that's vulnerable to physical or cyber attack. In addition to supporting confidentiality, encryption can play a role in other security tasks that will be discussed in the next few chapters, such as authenticating computer users, ensuring the integrity and authenticity of electronic information, and holding users accountable for their actions.

WHAT IS ENCRYPTION?

Simply put, encryption is the art and science of secret writing. Its purpose is to prevent unauthorized people from being able to understand a piece of information, even if it's right in front of them. Encryption has been used for thousands of years to protect business, political, and personal information. Julius Caesar and Thomas Jefferson both invented and used encryption systems to protect their sensitive communications.

The simplest encryption system involves an encryption algorithm (or process) and a single key. The encryption algorithm uses a key to change understandable information, such as a message, into a form that no one can understand. The encryption algorithm can then use the same key to descramble it. This kind of encryption is called symmetric because the same key is used to both encrypt and decrypt information.

Encryption keys are long numbers. A typical 128-bit key, named for the number of zeros and ones it has, looks like this:

11010010101010000011101010101010001011000111010101010110101
01100110100001011010101011010100010101101111101001110101010
10100010110001

or this:

2345AD0F1E34CF5B

Since it's not practical for people to type long strings of numbers when they need to unlock encrypted information, one approach is to enter a password. Transparent to the user, a password can be transformed into an encryption key that can either decrypt the information directly or decrypt other keys that can decrypt the information. In this situation, you can think of the password as protection for the key. If someone finds out what the password is, he'll have access to the key.

Another type of encryption, public key encryption, uses two keys. Information encrypted with one key, called a public key, can be decrypted only by the other key in the pair, the private key. (Appendix A contains more information on how encryption works.)

When using encryption, you are not eliminating a security problem; rather, you are trading one problem for another. You are trading the problem of protecting information for the problem of protecting the key you used to encrypt the information. The reasoning is that it is easier to protect the key than it is to protect the information encrypted with the key. By analogy, it is easier to lock the door to your home to prevent theft than it is to bolt every piece of furniture or stereo equipment to the floor. Relying on a locked door doesn't mean you no longer have security concerns about your personal belongings. It means you have traded the problem of protecting each chair and speaker for the problem of protecting your house key.

HOW ENCRYPTION PROTECTS BUSINESS PRIVACY

Let's look at how encryption can protect information confidentiality in certain business situations. The first situation is when information travels across networks. As discussed in chapter 2, hackers can intercept transmissions over the Internet and gather important business information. But the Internet isn't the only network that poses a threat to company information. A company's own internal networks can as well. Within an intranet, people can configure computers to operate in what's known as "promiscuous mode," meaning that they will be able to read information traveling across the internal network, even if it wasn't intended for them. Even companies that set up their networks to prevent this promiscuous activity are still vulnerable to well-known hacker techniques.

Other business situations that warrant encryption protection involve information stored on a computer. While computers will continue to be stolen from offices, businesses in most cases can mitigate this risk through physical security measures such as locked rooms and steel cables. One physical environment over which businesses have little control, though, is that of a laptop. Laptop theft is one of the most common types of physical attacks on businesses today. According to an insurance industry survey, 591,000 laptops were stolen in 2001, up 53 percent from 2000.[2]

One way to protect against the loss of confidential business information due to stolen laptops is to encrypt the information stored on a laptop. What that means is the user must enter a password when turning on the laptop. The password is then converted to a key that will decrypt the information on the laptop. This approach to protecting sensitive information has been used for years by such organizations as Amnesty International, which uses encryption to protect the names and lives of people who report human rights abuses.[3] A laptop thief will not be able to steal the information on the laptop if he doesn't have the password used to generate the key.

Another reason to use encryption is a lack of trust in a computer's ability to resist a digital attack. Even if a computer has a firewall and other security protections, it can still be broken into. Encryption can provide a second level of defense, so that even if someone breaks into a computer, sensitive information remains private. If a company is operating an e-commerce Web site, for example, it would be prudent to encrypt the credit card numbers that are stored on Web site computers.

Lack of trust in the employees who administer company computers is also a good reason for using encryption. Applications such as enterprise resource planning (ERP), customer relationship management (CRM), and database management systems (DBMS) contain some of an organization's most sensitive data. While these applications control what information ordinary employees are permitted to access, information technology staffers often have administrative access. This means that, in many cases, administrators can see and modify all data within an application without detection.

Although businesses are willing to trust administrators to perform the routine tasks to keep their applications up and running, they don't necessarily trust them not to abuse unlimited power. Encryption provides an additional layer of protection that administrators can't bypass. The use of encryption in this situation does not eliminate the need to trust administrators; rather, it shifts this trust to a different type of administrator, usually one whose responsibility is security. Regardless of how encryption keys are managed, there must be a set of administrators who have access to the keys. You should know whom in your company you're trusting with the keys—and then limit that group of people to a manageable number.

When a company decides which information assets it will encrypt, it should enter them in the information asset table (table 5-1). This data, in conjunction with other data such as current access permissions, will enable a company to quickly see how it is protecting its information assets. This is useful both during internal company security audits as well as during external security reviews, such as those for regulatory compliance or those requested by prospective customers or partners.

TABLE 5-1

Information Asset Table: Storage Encryption

Asset Name	Storage Encryption
Term sheet for a corporate acquisition	Yes
Customer record	No
Company phone book	No

One important point to remember is that businesses need to make sure keys are available when they're needed to decrypt information. Consider the situation in which an individual employee, not an administrator, can decide what information, such as a financial report for a potential corporate acquisition, is encrypted on a company computer. The only way to access the report is to have the key. If the employee who wrote the report is the only one with the key, then access to the report depends on access to the employee. This is fine if the employee is available whenever the report is needed. But what happens if the employee can't be reached because he's in transit on an overseas business trip, on vacation, or, in the worst-case scenario, hit by a bus? To account for these kinds of situations, companies need to have in place security technologies and procedures, often called key backup, that ensure they have continuous access to every key used to encrypt company information.

HOW ENCRYPTION CAN FAIL

Three factors can limit the effectiveness of encryption: mismanagement of keys, design flaws, and programming errors. While these vulnerabilities may sound overly technical, they are relatively simple to understand and can have powerful consequences.

As mentioned before, encryption doesn't eliminate a security problem—it only shifts it elsewhere. Customer information, such as credit card numbers, is safe only if the key that encrypted it is safe. Protecting keys is a large part of managing them. Unfortunately, many companies store the keys they use to encrypt sensitive information in text files on the same computer as the information these keys encrypt. Why is that a problem? Companies use encryption in this situation to guard against hackers who can take over their computers and bypass the security protections that would otherwise protect their information. But if a hacker can access every file on a computer, he can access the file containing the key. Using encryption to protect credit card numbers and other sensitive information on company computers won't be effective if the keys are as vulnerable to attack as the information they are supposedly protecting.

Another way an attacker can gain access to encrypted information is to exploit a design flaw in the encryption algorithm itself. Encryption algorithms and protocols combine to form the software instructions behind encryption. Think of encryption algorithms as ingredients and encryption protocols as recipes. A cook needs both good ingredients and a kitchen-tested recipe in order to prepare a good meal. Similarly, a company needs both well-designed encryption algorithms and protocols to protect the confidentiality of its information. A design flaw could allow encrypted data to be recovered with little effort. For example, in 1997 researchers found a design flaw in the algorithm used to encrypt cellular telephone calls in the United States, which meant anyone with a computer and a scanner could listen in on supposedly private conversations.[4] In 1999, the discovery of a design flaw in the copy protection encryption in DVD-audio players caused Matsushita Electric Industrial Co. and JVC to delay the launch of their new products, missing out on the lucrative Christmas season.[5]

Even if encryption algorithms and protocols are designed correctly, security vulnerabilities can be introduced through programming errors or "bugs." All software has bugs, and so it is reasonable to assume that all encryption software has bugs, too. Individual bugs may or may not compromise security, but it is important to realize that they can.

Creating encryption algorithms is extremely complex because of the intricate mathematics and analysis involved, and it's difficult to detect design flaws. That's why it is important for companies to protect their information with well-known encryption algorithms that have undergone extensive outside review.

To mitigate the risk of programming and design mistakes, companies should purchase encryption products only from companies that have ongoing support for their products and use well-tested and analyzed encryption algorithms (see appendix A). Although this advice may seem obvious, many *Fortune* 500 companies use home-grown encryption. Often, the problem arises because the people making decisions about which encryption algorithm or program to use are computer programmers who will use them in their applications. Their thoughts center on getting it free, so they don't have to go through corporate purchasing approval, or getting it now, so they don't fall behind schedule. They don't, in general, think about the implications for the company as a whole if the encryption fails.

HOW ACME HANDLES ENCRYPTION

At the close of chapter 2, ACME had gone through the process of locating its information assets and determining how someone can get to them. Now ACME is ready to select encryption technologies to protect those assets.

One troublesome situation for ACME is that IT staffers at headquarters are using dial-up connections to manage computers in field offices. These dial-up connections are not encrypted, so any attacker who intercepts a connection can grab the username and password that the IT administrator used to log on to the remote computer. At this point, an attacker could take complete control over the computers in a remote office.

As a short-term measure, the IT department decides to upgrade to the current release of the application it uses for managing remote computers. This release includes a feature to encrypt all of the information transmitted between IT computers at headquarters and computers in each field office and factory. This solution is relatively inexpensive and can be deployed quickly without affecting other parts of the company's computer infrastructure.

As a longer-term measure, the ACME security team decides it wants to protect the confidentiality of all network communication between headquarters and field offices. To accomplish this, they will look at combining encryption with firewalls. ACME has a firewall at headquarters, but protection at all of the sales offices and manufacturing facilities is a mixed bag. Some have firewalls, but others don't, and the firewalls that are in place come from various vendors. The security team decides to install firewalls at all offices that don't have them and upgrade existing firewalls, as necessary, so they all support virtual private network (VPN) connections to the other firewalls. A VPN encrypts all of the information that travels through it, so even though the information is traveling over the Internet, it's private and protected from eavesdroppers. This security technology provides ACME with the trust evidence it needs to meet its trust objective of maintaining the confidentiality of its information assets while they are transmitted between offices via the Internet.

The second issue concerns remote access to company computers by traveling employees and employees working from home. Currently, employees use vulnerable dial-up connections that are so busy at times that some employees can't connect to do work. Plus, employees rack up long-distance charges while traveling. ACME addresses this situation by extending the encryption capabilities of its firewalls to support VPNs for individual employees. Instead of dialing up to connect to a company computer, employees dial a local phone number to connect to the Internet, and then use the Internet to connect to the company's firewall. The VPN encrypts all information between the employee's computer or laptop and a company firewall.

The primary motivation for this use of encryption is to ensure the confidentiality of sensitive business information traveling to and from remote employees. Additional benefits include eliminating the security vulnerability of dial-up access points into corporate computers and saving money on long-distance telephone bills. One potential limitation of this approach is that an employee has to have VPN software installed on her desktop or laptop computer, so she can't use other computers, such as those in hotel business centers, to make a secure connection. ACME executives and the security team decide this is a reasonable limitation and create a policy that all traveling and remote employees have to use computers that have VPN capabilities when connecting to the company's internal network.

The second situation concerning traveling employees is defending against information disclosure as a result of laptop theft. The initial proposal was to install encryption programs on every laptop that would automatically encrypt and decrypt information, based on the laptop user's password-derived encryption key. The problem that ACME faces is what to do if someone forgets his or her password or becomes disgruntled and leaves ACME without telling anyone her or his password. The result in both cases is that ACME would no longer have access to ACME information. As a result, the security team decides to table this issue until it looks at other trust objectives that could use encryption so they can address all of their encryption requirements in an integrated way.

The last type of communication ACME addresses is e-mail. Much of ACME's most sensitive information is transmitted via e-mail, both within the company and externally. ACME doesn't have an e-mail standard, so ACME employees use various e-mail programs, and the companies with which ACME communicates use different e-mail programs as well. Given the complexity of this scenario, the security team decides to deploy a quick solution for critical situations, such as the need to share engineering information with the partner company that is designing the new motor for ACME. This involves the use of encryption programs that create self-decrypting files. Such programs are inexpensive (a version from the Massachusetts Institute of Technology is actually free[6]), easy to use, and don't require IT support for set up.

When someone wants to send a file with sensitive information, she enters a password and the encryption program encrypts the file with a key derived from the password. At that point the person can send the encrypted file as an e-mail attachment. When the e-mail arrives, the recipient can call the sender for the password and use it to open and decrypt the file. Even though telephone calls can be tapped, this is a safe practice for companies most of the time because it's a much more difficult task for an attacker to intercept and correlate information from both the Internet and the telephone system. For greater security, the sender and receiver can agree on a password in person.

Although this encryption solution can work on a small scale, it's too cumbersome for use across all of ACME. For a companywide solution, the security team proposes using an Internet standard for e-mail encryption called S/MIME, since over thirty e-mail programs can be enabled to support S/MIME.[7] Using it for encrypting e-mail involves only a small amount of extra work for users, so ACME hopes there will be minimal resistance to this new security technology. However, since encryption may be valuable for protecting other information assets, the security team decides to postpone making a final decision on an S/MIME vendor or product until it examines other uses for encryption as it continues through the corporate security process. The administration of S/MIME can be quite complex and time consuming so the security team will conduct a small trial in the IT department before making the final decision to deploy S/MIME throughout the entire company. The use of S/MIME to protect e-mail communications between ACME and other companies would then require collaboration between IT administrators at ACME and these other companies.[8]

SIX

Establishing Identity

Imagine how impossible it would be to conduct business safely if you didn't know the other party in the deal. You could do simple things like fork over a few quarters for a newspaper on a street corner, but that's about it. Fortunately, you can get ample evidence, such as an introduction by a mutual colleague, to assure yourself that the person you are talking to is actually the person you think he is. In the digital world, however, much of this evidence is not available, and businesspeople are left with the difficult decision of whether they should conduct business with a name displayed on their computer monitor.

This chapter covers the security technologies and practices that provide the necessary evidence for the second trust objective: trusting the digital identities of individuals and organizations. Although most of the chapter will address personal digital identities, such as an employee's username for a computer application, the same issues apply to organizational identities, such as Web site addresses. In either case, businesses need to pay attention to two distinct but related processes in order to trust digital identities: creating the identity and authenticating the identity. Think of the creation process as the issuance of familiar types of identification, such as driver's licenses, passports, library cards, and grocery club cards, and the authentication process as a passport check when entering a country.

Although they sound elementary, these two processes, called identification and authentication (I&A), involve some of the trickiest information security problems. Why? For most people, entering a username and password to log on to a computer or application is the most visible and intrusive information security mechanism they encounter. Because this act of authenticating a digital identity is so common, many of the security issues surrounding the *creation* of digital identities are overlooked.

CREATING DIGITAL IDENTITIES

Digital identities can be created by a business, such as an employee's company; an Internet service provider (ISP) that provides a network connection to the Internet; or an online application vendor, such as an airline reservation Web site. The degree to which businesspeople and their companies can trust digital identities depends on how well the business that created the identity performs two tasks:

- verifying a person's real-world identity, and

- creating and protecting the evidence for authenticating the person's digital identity.

The amount of real-world identity evidence a business gathers before issuing a digital identity varies according to the business's own needs. For example, businesses that provide free e-mail, such as Yahoo! Mail, don't require any proof of a person's real-world identity before issuing him a username to access the e-mail service. The person can choose the first part of his e-mail address, which is the "name" part of name@yahoo.com, and the name doesn't have to have any connection to the person's real name. Since the service is free, the e-mail provider doesn't have to collect and verify any personal information about its users. This business situation is similar to that of grocery stores that issue frequent-shopping cards. There's no security risk because the cards can't be used to buy anything.

At the other end of the spectrum is the process companies go through when issuing digital identities to new employees. By the time an employee is hired, the company has interviewed the employee, checked professional references, and, in some cases, checked criminal and driving records. In short, the company knows who the employee is when it issues digital identifiers such as a username for company applications and an e-mail address. The amount of due diligence a company performs in establishing an employee's real-world identity more closely resembles the process for issuing a passport than a grocery club card.

The other part of creating a digital identity is creating and protecting the evidence—typically a password—that a person will use to authenticate that identity. The primary concern is how the issuing business protects the evidence while it is stored and while it is transmitted between a user and the application authenticating the user. Although it is standard security practice to encrypt passwords that travel over the Internet, many companies and online applications don't encrypt passwords consistently, or at all. For example, one popular enterprise application encrypts passwords when users log on, but not when they change their passwords. Another enterprise commerce application does encrypt changed passwords, but negates this protection by sending unencrypted e-mail to confirm these new passwords. Similarly, the protections companies afford stored passwords vary significantly. Some companies encrypt passwords on computers that they protect with firewalls and intrusion detection, while other companies provide little protection.

A lack of protection for authentication evidence undercuts a company's trust in the validity of digital identities. Does this username or e-mail address really belong to the person who is using it?

AUTHENTICATING DIGITAL IDENTITIES

Authenticating a digital identity involves two tasks: determining that the digital identity is valid and that the digital identity's owner is the person using it. Verifying the validity of a digital identity is straightforward when a person is logging on to a company application. All the application has to do is check to see if the person's username is on the list of valid accounts. This is similar to checking a person's name on the guest list at a party.

Determining that a digital identity belongs to the person trying to use it consists of comparing the authentication evidence the person provides to the evidence created when the digital identity was established. Authentication evidence falls into three basic categories commonly called factors:

- something a person *knows,*

- something a person *has,* and

- something a person *is.*

Each of these factors, alone or in combination with others, can be an effective and appropriate means for authentication. However, the security and practicality of different types of authentication evidence are not always clear. Companies should make sure they know the value of various kinds of authentication evidence when selecting technical solutions for themselves and evaluating the solutions of partner companies.

Evidence a Person Knows

Something a user *knows* is far and away the most common form of authentication evidence in use today, and will continue to be for a long time. The most common example of authentication evidence a person knows is a password. Variants include Personal Identification Numbers (PINs) and pass phrases, which are made up of several passwords.

Passwords are easy to use, don't require special hardware, and can be used from any computer. When a person enters her username and password, the application compares the entered password with the one it has on file for the username. If they match, the user is authenticated and can access the application. A password protects the use of a digital identity in the same way that a key protects the information encrypted with it. Passwords have the same confidentiality requirements that keys do.

Unlike encryption keys, people need to remember passwords, and there is a natural tendency to use familiar information, such as a pet's name or a birthday, as a password. While this approach makes remembering a password easier, it also simplifies an attacker's task of guessing a password. With the advent of online dictionaries, the use of ordinary words as passwords has become problematic because an attacker can automate the process of trying to match a password against every word in a dictionary.

Companies can promote better password security through the enforcement of policies such as requiring a minimum password length; requiring passwords to contain both numbers and letters; locking a user's account after a certain number of failed logon attempts; and requiring users to change their password periodically.[1] The automatic generation of hard-to-guess passwords, however, is a practice that usually results in decreased password security because people can't remember them and therefore write them down.

Evidence a Person Has

Even with all of these efforts to ensure password confidentiality, passwords are still guessed and stolen. When that happens, someone may not be aware that his password has been compromised until after the fact, if at all. This is a motivation for using a token, or an authentication factor that a person *has*. When employed as authentication evidence, tokens are most commonly used in conjunction with other evidence the user knows, such as a password or PIN. To impersonate someone who is using this kind of two-factor authentication requires knowing the password and having physical possession of the token. Even if an attacker accomplishes this, his window of opportunity will close as soon as the user discovers that his token is missing and contacts an administrator to revoke the old token and issue a new one.

Businesses today use two principal types of tokens: password-generating tokens and smart cards. The first type of token generates dynamic passwords. In one common model, the token displays a random password that changes regularly. The user enters his username, regular password, and the dynamic password currently displayed on the token. The system knows which token belongs to which user and knows if the dynamic password is valid for this user at that time. One of the operational advantages of password-generating tokens is that they don't require any special hardware and therefore can be used at any computer. Many companies, including a major U.S. online brokerage firm, use password-generating tokens for authenticating staff who manage and maintain their computer systems.

Smart cards, on the other hand, are very small computers that can not only store information, as in the magnetic stripes on credit cards, but also perform tasks. A user generally enters a PIN to access the smart card, another example of two-factor authentication. Because of memory capacity, smart cards can also contain information about the holder, such as medical history, in addition to authentication evidence.

One limitation on the use of smart cards is that they require a smart card reader to work. At present very few computers are equipped with smart card readers, although availability will improve over time. Smart card use in the United States has traditionally lagged behind Europe, where, for example, Netherlands-based Royal Dutch Shell issued smart cards to all of its nearly one hundred thousand employees. Adoption in the United States is growing, with 41 million smart cards manufactured in 2001 for U.S. use, a 45 percent increase over the previous year. In addition, the U.S. Department of Defense is rolling out 4.3 million smart cards to military and civilian employees and contractors.[2]

Biometric Evidence

The third factor used for authentication is something the user *is,* also known as a biometric. A biometric is an observable physical characteristic that is unique to each person. Fingerprints and retinal scans are common forms of biometrics, but voice patterns and face and hand geometry are used as well. Unlike passwords that can be forgotten or tokens that can be misplaced, people don't leave their thumbs on the kitchen table. As with smart cards, biometric evidence, such as a fingerprint, is entered into a reader or scanner. When a person puts his thumb in a thumbprint reader, the analog picture of his thumb is converted to a digital one and compared against the digital image on his record for a match.

Biometrics differ from other authentication evidence in three ways: secrecy, revocability, and accuracy. The effectiveness of the first two types of authentication evidence discussed depends on keeping the evidence—for example, a password—secret. On the other hand, biometrics, especially fingerprints, are not secrets. There are many situations in which people are fingerprinted, even if they are not criminals, such as buying a house or getting a driver's license. It is impossible to know where all of these fingerprints are or how well they are protected.

Another way in which biometrics differ from other authentication factors is that they can't be revoked. If someone figures out your password, you can revoke it and get a new one. The same holds true for a smart card. What do you do if someone steals the image of your right thumbprint from one of the computers on which it is stored? Revoking your right thumb isn't a good option.

The last way in which biometrics differ from other authentication evidence is that they are not precise. The conversion process from analog to digital can introduce errors, as can a change in a scanned body part, such as a thumb that is cut, callused, or bruised. This imprecision can result in denying access to legitimate users and authenticating impostors.

The argument is often put forward that fingerprints and other biometrics are the most secure type of authentication evidence because each one is unique. This argument misses the point because the security of validating digital identities with biometrics doesn't depend on biometrics being unique. It depends on the owner of a biometric being the only one who can use it as authentication evidence. That can be as difficult a task as protecting the confidentiality of other authentication evidence.

USING DIGITAL CERTIFICATES

Digital certificates embody a different approach to creating and authenticating digital identities that is built on public key encryption. Systems using digital certificates are often called public key infrastructures (PKI). As stated in chapter 5, public key encryption uses public/private key pairs such that anything encrypted with one of the keys can be decrypted only by its mate. A digital certificate is an electronic record that contains information such as the certificate holder's name, a serial number, validity period, the holder's company name and address, and a public key created for use in the certificate. The private key created at the same time is encrypted for its protection and stored on the certificate holder's computer.

Why use digital certificates? One reason is to make it easier for companies to provide multiple services to their users, who may include their own employees and customers as well as the employees of other companies and organizations. Most computer users have numerous digital identities, often one for each application or service they use. A digital identity created for one application frequently can't be used for another application. Think of the number of different accounts you have for Internet services, such as banking, travel reservations, e-mail, and news services. A digital certificate that is created once can be used by multiple applications, increasing convenience while at the same time reducing the administrative overhead of maintaining multiple digital identities. Another reason for using digital certificates is that they offer a more precise description of how well they can be trusted than other digital identities do. This is because certificate authorities publish the rules and procedures they follow for validating real-world identities. In addition, digital certificates are required for other encryption applications, such as S/MIME.

The process of creating a digital certificate begins when the certificate requestor presents evidence of his real-world identity to a certificate authority for validation. Certificate authorities are commercial and government organizations that verify people's real-world identities and then issue digital certificates that these people can use as digital identities. A certificate authority's function is similar to that of a motor vehicle department that verifies a person's identity before issuing him a driver's license.

After verifying the requestor's identity and collecting the information that goes into a digital certificate, a certificate authority digitally "signs" the certificate. This encryption operation protects the certificate from tampering, because once it's signed, even the smallest change in the certificate can be detected.

There are two parts to the process of authenticating a user with a digital certificate. First, the signature must be verified to detect tampering. Then it must be verified that the digital certificate belongs to the person presenting it. Let's say a hospital application is verifying that a digital certificate belongs to a doctor before allowing him to update medication instructions for his patients. The application can use the public key in the doctor's digital certificate to encrypt a secret number and send it to the doctor's computer. The doctor enters a password to decrypt his private key (which in turn decrypts the secret number), and then his computer sends back the number plus one, proving to the hospital application that it's really the doctor who's logging on. For increased security, other evidence, such as tokens, smart cards, and biometrics, can be used to protect the private key.

WHEN DIGITAL IDENTITIES GO BAD

If it all sounds too complicated, remember what was said at the beginning of the chapter: Entering a username and password to log on to a computer or application is the most visible and intrusive information security mechanism people encounter. It's so common that many businesses, even those that are security-conscious, still get caught by surprise when someone breaches their system.

Thirty-one-year-old Brooklyn busboy Abraham Abdallah was a master of online impersonation.[3] Abdallah pretended he was Thomas Siebel, the billionaire founder of software company Siebel Systems, as well as Oprah Winfrey, Michael Eisner, George Lucas, and Michael Bloomberg.

But the impersonation didn't stop there. New York City police and federal investigators told the *New York Times* that Abdallah acquired publicly available Social Security numbers, birth dates, and mothers' maiden names for 217 people on the *Forbes* magazine list of the richest people in the United States. Using this information, he was able to set up fraudulent credit cards under these billionaires' names, which he used to charge more than $100,000 in luxury goods. He then used that information to order credit history reports. Employing the "social engineering" techniques mentioned earlier, he was able to trick employees at banks and brokerage firms into giving him passwords that controlled accounts. He also established phony Yahoo! e-mail addresses to impersonate the superrich, which were later found linked to these people's personal accounts at Merrill Lynch, Bear Stearns, and Goldman Sachs. His impersonation career ended when he allegedly tried to transfer $10 million from a Merrill Lynch account belonging to Thomas Siebel. The only reason an alarm went off was that the withdrawal would have caused Siebel's account to become overdrawn.

Abdallah's success was largely due to two factors. He used digital identities, such as Yahoo! e-mail addresses, that companies, including Merrill Lynch, Bear Stearns, and Goldman Sachs, trusted even though there was no basis for that trust. And many of the financial institutions involved in this case use authentication evidence, such as Social Security numbers, that are not secret. This case is not an example of broken or flawed security technology or even a sophisticated hacker attack. Rather, it demonstrates the consequences when companies don't understand what it takes to establish the necessary trust in a digital identity.

Business use of authentication evidence such as Social Security numbers and mothers' maiden names to validate customers' identities contributes to the ever-increasing problem of identity theft. These bits of personal information are not secret, because information used as a digital identifier in one context can also be used as authentication evidence in another. For example, many health insurance companies use Social Security numbers to identify their customers, while banks and credit card companies use the last four digits of a Social Security number as authentication evidence. What's more, these types of authenticators can't be revoked once they've been compromised. A mother's maiden name will remain the same regardless of how many people know it. The Federal Trade Commission received more than three thousand calls a week related to identity theft in 2002.[4] Even though individuals are the most obvious victims of identity theft, there is a cost to businesses, as well. Banks, credit card companies, and merchants must write off the bad debt that identity thieves create.

Sometimes an attacker doesn't even have to steal an entire identity to cause problems. Simply compromising passwords can be enough to cause serious damage. In July 2002, Jay Berlin, a manager at Nike Corp., received a call from a salesperson at Business Engine Software Corp.[5] It was surprising, because he'd never heard of the firm and his job doesn't involve buying the kind of Internet collaboration software Business Engine sells. He did some investigating and found that Business Engine was a prime competitor of Niku Corp., the company where Berlin's brother-in-law Warren Leggett is CIO. Berlin had agreed to let Leggett make a product presentation at Nike and somehow, Berlin and Leggett realized, Business Engine had found out. Leggett reviewed Niku's Web access logs and discovered that someone at a computer owned by Business Engine used fifteen passwords belonging to Niku employees to download around one thousand documents, including one Leggett wrote about the Nike sales call. With further digging, Leggett discovered that someone outside of the company secretly had been stealing sensitive information assets for over half a year. The stolen information included upcoming features, potential customer lists, and pricing.

Referring to the way the information theft was discovered, Niku chief executive Farzad Dibachi said, "It was sheer coincidence. Otherwise, who knows how long this would have gone on?" Well, it shouldn't have gone on for very long at all. Even if employee passwords are stolen, there are measures a company can take to minimize the damage. The first thing Niku should have done was review its Web logs frequently. Many companies do this already, both to identify potential customers as well as competitors and to see what they are interested in. Niku might have noticed Business Engine's activity long before it caused problems. The next thing Niku should have done was make employees periodically change their passwords, so stolen passwords couldn't be used forever. A third helpful measure would be to display a message when a user logs on indicating the last time he was logged on. This can alert a user that someone else is using his account. These are just a few measures Niku and other companies can take to minimize the effects of a competitor's attack.

IDENTITY ISSUES WITH OTHER COMPANIES

So far, we've discussed some of the issues companies face in dealing with individual digital identities. There are also significant issues when companies do business with each other.

An example based on real-world business-to-business (B2B) on-line trade exchanges illustrates how businesses have approached the problem of trusting each other in order to buy and sell indirect and direct goods (see figure 6-1).

Examples of indirect goods are office supplies and paper products that a company uses but are not directly related to the products and services it sells. Headlights and mufflers are examples of direct goods for an automobile manufacturer. Figure 6-1 shows three organizations: the exchange, a supplier, and a buyer. The exchange acts both as a matchmaker between trading partners and as an environment in which these organizations can conduct business.

FIGURE 6-1

B2B Exchange

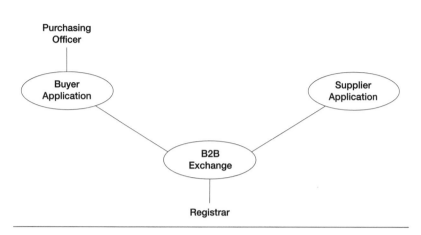

In its matchmaker role, the exchange is responsible for registering all of its trading partners and creating unique digital identities they can use within the exchange. Registration includes performing a due diligence review of each trading partner to verify that the company is what it purports to be and has a history of paying its bills promptly. One way of accomplishing this is to obtain a Dun & Bradstreet report about the company.

In a simple transaction, a purchasing officer for the buying organization needs to buy ten thousand packages of paper towels. The purchasing officer uses his company's buying application to order the paper towels. The buying application sends a request to the exchange application for the lowest-cost paper supplier. When it finds the best price, the exchange application returns this information to the buying application, which then sends a purchase order through the exchange to the chosen paper company. The paper supplier's application receives and processes the purchase order, and takes care of billing and fulfillment.

Looking at this transaction from the supplier's perspective, there are three authentication processes that must take place securely in order for the supplier to trust the origin of the purchase order:

1. The purchasing officer authenticates himself to his company's buyer application to submit the purchase order.

2. The buyer application authenticates its identity to the exchange when sending the purchase order to the exchange.

3. The exchange authenticates itself to the supplier application when forwarding the purchase order.

The supplier organization has no control over any aspect of the first two authentication processes, nor does it have control over how the exchange protects its own authentication evidence in step three. The way in which the trade exchange addresses this lack of control is by promulgating security standards that all trading partners, and the exchange itself, have to meet. These standards cover the creation of personal and digital identities as well as the choice and protection of authentication evidence. The trade exchange audits compliance with these standards and has a range of punitive measures to address noncompliance.

This trade exchange example highlights two areas in which companies need to rethink their approach to digital identities as they move from a company-centric model to a collaborative model. The first area is satisfying a company's trust requirements for digital identity creation and authentication when parts or all of these processes are no longer under the company's control. The second area is meeting a company's requirements for knowing with whom it is transacting business. In some contexts, it may be an employee of another company and in others it could be a computer program acting on behalf of another company. This ambiguity makes it difficult for a company to decide if it should honor a purchase order or invoice it receives.

Although helpful, security technology doesn't provide all of the solutions for addressing these new situations. The solutions can be found in traditional business agreements that specify the rights and responsibilities of each party in a business relationship. In order to know what terms to include in these agreements, companies need to clearly understand and articulate their own trust objectives.

SELECTING IDENTIFICATION AND
AUTHENTICATION TECHNOLOGY

When companies select I&A technologies, they should balance the amount of security they need with the amount of security they can bear. To determine how much authentication security a company needs, it should look at the value of the information assets users will be able to access once they've logged on. This information valuation doesn't have to be an elaborate or detailed process because the number of basic I&A choices is small. From a pure security perspective, passwords are more appropriate for authenticating users of low-sensitivity information and two-factor authentication using tokens or biometrics is more appropriate for authenticating users of high-sensitivity information. Digital certificates use two-factor authentication and are appropriate for access to high-sensitivity information, especially in cases where a company wants to use encryption for other purposes, such as protecting e-mail or the information on laptops.

Another point to remember is that companies don't have to use the same I&A solution for all of their users. For example, many companies require their IT staff to authenticate themselves using a password and a token-generated one-time password, while regular employees only need to enter a password. An attacker with access to an IT administrative account could bring down a company's entire computing infrastructure, while an attacker who has broken into a regular user's account is restricted by that user's permissions.

In addition to information value, another criterion that companies use for selecting authentication solutions is the degree of risk that an attacker could impersonate a legitimate user. In general, this can translate into using a weaker type of authentication evidence, such as a password, when a user logs on inside a company office; and using stronger, two-factor authentication evidence when a user logs on remotely.

The amount of protection a company provides its information assets is based, in part, on the strength of the authentication evidence users must present in order to log on to a computer or application to access the assets. This information, called "current authentication," goes into the information asset table (see table 6-1). In two of the examples in the table, passwords are the required authentication evidence because the assets have lower value. For the term sheet, digital certificates with token-protected private keys are the required authentication evidence. That's because of its high sensitivity. The information asset table also includes a column called "available authentication," which indicates what other options exist for authentication. Information entered in this column will be helpful in the future should security priorities change in a way that impacts authentication strength.

Having decided which authentication technology a company needs, the next task is determining how much of this technology a company can realistically deploy. Companies can easily perform this task by asking how much inconvenience they can impose on their users in terms of extra procedures, hardware, and software. Companies have the most control over their own employees, which works out well since employee accounts have the greatest access to company information assets. However, companies have much less control over their customers; and customers who feel that it is too difficult to do business with one company will switch to another one, unless there is a compelling reason to stay.

TABLE 6-1

Information Asset Table: Current and Available Authentication

Asset Name	Current Authentication	Available Authentication
Term sheet for a corporate acquisition	Digital certificate, token-protected private key	Password, digital certificate, password and token-protected private key
Customer record	Password	Password, digital certificate, password and token-protected private key
Company phone book	Password	Password, digital certificate, password and token-protected private key

Another potential form of user inconvenience is the need to have specific software or hardware on users' computers in order to authenticate themselves. Some applications, such as those that banks provide for large industrial clients to manage their accounts, require the installation of programs on users' computers. Smart card and biometric-based authentication requires the installation of hardware readers and scanners, the cost of which has to be considered. In addition, users won't be able to log on from computers without these readers, which is problematic for people who use public computers, such as those in hotel business centers, airports, and libraries. Before deploying an authentication system, companies should first determine if their customers will be able and willing to use it.

And then there is single sign-on (SSO), one of the holy grails of corporate information security. Often there are too many passwords for employees to remember, so they write them down, further exposing their companies to attack. Using the same password for all accounts isn't possible because different applications have different rules regarding what a password needs to look like. An employee's desire to enter one password at the beginning of the day and be able to do all of her work without entering another password is quite strong. It's also a largely unsatisfied desire.

This is because most enterprise applications, especially older ones, authenticate users themselves. Thus companies face the impossible task of convincing all of their application vendors to change their products to work in a single sign-on environment in which a single password unlocks all applications. Companies can approach this problem from two angles. The first is to make support for single sign-on a requirement for all new applications. To supplement this, companies can use security applications that keep track of all employees' accounts and passwords on all company applications. After an employee logs on to the security application, it automatically logs the employee onto the rest of the applications he needs. The one security caveat for single sign-on is that a hacker can now access more information with one compromised password than he could before.

HOW ACME HANDLES IDENTIFICATION AND AUTHENTICATION

The security team starts its examination of identification and authentication with a few priorities that have come from discussions with senior management. One priority is the ability to support different authentication strengths, depending on the value of the assets that can be accessed and on the potential risk of a hacker breaking into a user account. Another is to plan for more development collaborations similar to the current project with the motor company. Specifically, management wants to move away from the current practice of e-mailing design and engineering diagrams to another company because ACME loses control over the protection of that intellectual property. Instead, they want a model where ACME's engineering diagrams remain on ACME computers and outside engineering teams work on them by logging on to one of ACME's computer-aided-design applications.

Addressing the first priority, the security team examines the use of variable strengths of authentication evidence by information asset. ACME consults its information asset table to find the applications that manage high- and medium-value assets. Most of the applications only support passwords, but some support tokens. The newer Web-based applications support digital certificates as well. The security team discovers that passwords, unfortunately, are the only option for most of the high-value assets.

Given this situation, the security team, in conjunction with administrators for these applications, turns on all of the password security features these applications have. These include setting a minimum password length of eight characters, requiring a number in a password, and forcing users to change passwords every three to six months. In addition, they start the practice of routinely trying to guess or crack passwords. To do this, they utilize programs that automatically try common passwords as well as entire dictionaries as part of the password cracking process. Whenever they crack a password, they send an e-mail to the user instructing him that he has to change his password.

To address the additional risk of a hacker taking over the ACME account of a traveling or remote user, the security team recommends the use of a one-time password-generating token for use with the VPN. At present, they don't recommend the use of two-factor authentication within ACME facilities, but advise that the issue be revisited in six months, at least with respect to administrators.

The security team examines the feasibility of issuing digital certificates to all employees for user authentication. Given that it would take a significant effort to modify ACME's applications to accept digital certificates, the team decides against issuing certificates for general company use. The security team has a long-term plan of extending the use of the digital certificates beyond S/MIME for other purposes, such as encrypting the information on laptops when the technology is more mature.

The last priority the security team addresses is the creation of logon accounts, or digital identities, for employees at the partner company working on the motor design. This involves a few authentication issues. The first is authenticating a motor company employee over a VPN into ACME's internal network and then authenticating him to the right application. In addition to authenticating the outside user, ACME has to control what that user can do. To begin with, the user should not be allowed to do anything inside ACME's internal network other than log on to the computer-aided-design application. Once the user logs on to the application, he should be allowed to access only the diagrams and figures he needs for his project.

Chapter 7 addresses the various options companies have for controlling who can get to their information assets.

SEVEN

Controlling Access in the Digital World

When it comes to information security, companies are often their own worst enemies. Consider this scenario: A *Fortune* 500 company in the chemical industry keeps all of its product designs and formulas in a database. To protect this extremely valuable information, the company stores this database on a computer that most employees don't even know exists, let alone have access to. So far, so good. But the research and development department that manages the database decides—in an effort to promote knowledge management—that all twenty thousand plus employees of the chemical company should have access to these formulas. The department sets up a search engine on the company's global intranet that bypasses all of the access controls protecting the formula database, enabling every employee to view the company's most significant trade secrets. All an employee has to do is type "formula" into a form on his browser and the search engine delivers the formulas directly to the employee's computer, anywhere in the world.

The good news is that the company's competitors don't appear to know just how easy it is to steal this proprietary information from the R&D database. The bad news is that employees aren't the only ones who could easily gain access to this treasure trove of data. Thousands of nonemployees and former employees, including employees who were fired, also have access to the internal Web site. About one-third of the login accounts that provide access to this company's internal network don't belong to people currently working for the company. They are logins for past employees, contractors, and vendors that have never been deleted.

Imagine the catastrophic danger facing the company if this story were true. Well, it is. I've changed enough details to hide the company's identity, but it's typical of what I've seen over the last two decades across a broad range of companies. Despite this company's best efforts to protect itself, it still had a gaping security hole. That's because it let individual employees make security decisions that had significant impact on the company, without any corporate direction or oversight.

WHO SHOULD GET ACCESS TO WHAT?

The third trust objective in the Trust Framework addresses the challenge of getting information to the people who need it to do their jobs, while at the same time keeping these business assets out of the wrong hands. Controlling access to a company's information assets isn't merely about protecting electronic copies of product plans and financial reports. Because online information is used to track inventory, process orders, and set production rates, controlling access to information assets is essential for protecting a company's physical assets as well. The Internet raises the stakes for companies because it makes access to information assets much faster and easier, resulting in even greater corporate damage if proper controls aren't exercised. Although not as visible as virus attacks or Web site defacements, the theft of proprietary information is the most expensive information security problem that companies face (see figure 7-1). By comparison, the cost to companies from virus attacks is less than a third of that amount.

FIGURE 7-1

Dollar Amount of Losses by Type of Attack

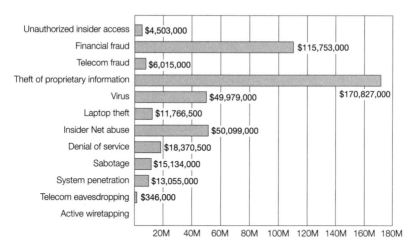

Source: Richard Power, "CSI/FBI 2002 Computer Crime and Security Survey," *Computer Security Issues & Trends* 8, no. 1 (2002): 14.

In this 2002 survey 223 respondents (44 percent) were able to quantify their losses by the type of attack.

The most important step a company can take to protect itself from the vulnerable situation described has little to do with information security technology, however. The answer is to develop an access control policy that defines which users are authorized to access which information assets. The process of determining who has access to company information assets, described in chapter 2, is the first step, because it defines what legitimate access to information assets already exists. If the company in the preceding example had gone through this process, it would have found the threat to its formulas and could have taken corrective action.

This chapter describes a variety of access control policies that companies can use to protect their information assets, along with some criteria companies should consider in selecting the right policy for them. Access control policies and their enforcement mechanisms address two specific threats. The first is a legitimate user who is trying to gain access to information he is not supposed to have or perform functions he's not authorized for. The second threat is a hacker who has broken into a legitimate user's account. One way of thinking about these two threats is to imagine you are throwing a holiday party at your company's headquarters for employees, partners, and customers. You have a doorman who checks that guests have invitations before letting them into the building, and the doorman then directs the guests to the room where the party is being held. You have a problem if some guests decide to start roaming around your offices, rifling through filing cabinets and pocketing sensitive documents. The problem grows more severe if a guest is not a guest at all, but instead a competitor who got past the doorman with an invitation he picked up off the sidewalk outside your building.

ACCESS BASED ON JOB FUNCTION

Companies often base their access control policies on job function. This approach has evolved significantly over the years in response to growing demand by companies for more control and flexibility in protecting their information assets. Consider the case of a growing company that has just arrived at the point where it needs a dedicated human resources (HR) department. The company has HR records, but until now it hasn't thought much about controlling access to them. The first task is to identify all information assets related to HR, which may be contained in individual files, directories of files, and databases. Once these HR assets, which might include employee medical and performance records as well as corporate policies, have been identified, the next task is to determine which of them are necessary for an HR staffer to do her job. Then an IT administrator grants the HR staffer the necessary file, directory, and database permissions to access the information she needs. The same process can be used for other HR staffers, who may need access to different HR information.

While granting access permissions on a user-by-user basis is manageable with a small number of employees, it is not feasible for an organization with hundreds or thousands of employees. One technique that businesses have used to accommodate larger user populations is called "cloning" accounts. Let's say that an employee has the set of access permissions that most HR staff need. Instead of determining the specific permissions a new employee needs, a typical HR employee's permissions can be cloned and granted to the new hire. The new employee may be missing some permissions he needs or have others he doesn't need, but one benefit of this approach is that he'll be productive more quickly than if he waited until an HR manager had time to determine the exact information assets he required.

ACCESS BASED ON EMPLOYEE ROLE

The informal practice of cloning permissions has evolved into direct application support for role-based access control policies. Although not universal, most enterprise applications, such as customer relationship management, database management, and enterprise resource planning, support access control policies based on the role an employee has within a company. Using roles to control access is a two-step process: first, defining what access permissions a role should have, and second, granting a user the roles he needs to do his work.

In most situations, it is helpful for companies to separate the functions of role definer and role granter, as this separation reduces the number of people who need a broad security understanding of company information assets. To define a role, a person must know what information an employee acting in a particular role needs, and what impact these access permissions would have on the rest of the company. By contrast, granting a role to an employee is an administrative task that does not require the same security and companywide perspective.

The National Institute of Standards and Technology (NIST), the U.S. government's lead agency for commercial information security, has promulgated an innovative use of roles that enforce policies centered on dynamic or static separation of duties.[1] A static separation of duties policy defines certain job functions that one employee should never have at the same time, such as working in a company's finance department and auditing the same finance department. By designating the finance and audit roles as a static separation of duties, an employee who has been granted the finance role can't be assigned the audit role, and vice versa. The only way for an employee to get the other role is if the first role and all of its access permissions are taken away first.

A dynamic separation of duties policy states that the same individual can be assigned two roles, but he can't use both at the same time. For example, consider a bank employee who has both a teller role and a teller supervisor role, where the supervisor role has the privilege to approve corrections to a teller's open cash drawer. To eliminate the opportunity for a supervisor to approve his own fraudulent teller activities, a dynamic separation of duties policy could require a bank employee to close his cash drawer and drop the teller role before assuming the teller supervisor role.

ACCESS BASED ON ETHICAL WALLS

An ethical wall, also known as a Chinese wall, is an example of an access control policy typically used in organizations such as law firms and banks that need a complete separation between different groups of employees and their work. For instance, law firms are legally obligated to turn down work to avoid a conflict of interest, even though their profitability depends on accepting as many new clients as they can handle. Under both state and federal ethics rules, a law firm cannot take on a new client if it would result in a conflict of interest with an existing client. For example, if a law firm is representing one company in a corporate litigation, the firm cannot then take on as a client the opposing company in the same litigation. However, if a law firm is handling patent work for the first company that has nothing to do with the litigation, a law firm could take on the new company, provided that both companies sign conflict of interest waivers.

When this happens, a law firm builds an ethical wall between the attorneys working for the two companies. Every piece of information dealing with a client, in paper as well as electronic form, is labeled with a client ID and a matter ID, such as litigation or patent. These IDs are then used as the basis for access control decisions so no information crosses the wall. When an attorney working on the litigation matter is ethically walled off from the other company's patent matter, access control technology and office procedures prevent him from accessing inappropriate information with the other company's patent label.

The success of this type of access control depends on the cooperation of all employees. In many firms, there is a general announcement alerting staff to a new ethical wall, so no one sends the walled-off attorney voicemail or e-mail containing prohibited information. The staff understands the consequences of not controlling access to walled-off information, which could include a mistrial, a law firm being removed from a case, a lawsuit, or a significant career setback for an attorney or paralegal.

Another example of an ethical wall can be found in banks that separate the group that invests the bank's money from the group that invests the bank's customers' money. An ethical wall was also used during merger talks between Hewlett-Packard and Compaq. Given the size and complexity of the merger, it was important to have a transition team in place as early as possible to map out organizational and product changes that would result. However, the companies were still competitors as the talks went on, so they built an ethical wall to separate the transition team from the two companies.

Companies can use a variety of security technologies and procedures to enforce ethical walls. For example, an accounting firm that maintains ethical walls between each of its customers could assign a different role to each of its accountants, where each role corresponds to a different client and all of the roles enforce a static separation of duties. Alternatively, an accounting firm could dedicate entirely separate computers to the processing of each client's taxes.

Although government regulations are often the reason companies erect ethical walls, enlightened self-interest—and the fallout from the collapse of Enron and Arthur Andersen—should provide motivation as well. Another high-visibility bankruptcy in 1995 resulted from a lack of separation between derivatives trading and back-office settlement.[2] Nicholas Leeson was able to disguise his massive losses from trading because he also had access to his bank's back-office settlement system. This resulted in the collapse of Baring Brothers & Co., Britain's oldest merchant bank.

CONTROLLING THE UNCONTROLLABLE

So far, this chapter has focused on how companies can control employees' access to information assets. But what can businesses do after employees get their hands on those assets? In most cases, they can't do much. Once an employee has access to information, the company must rely on his discretion and judgment in sharing or distributing the information. In principle, this is no different from how companies manage the release of paper documents. However, the speed and ease with which electronic information can be e-mailed anywhere in the world means that businesses today face a fundamentally larger risk that information will get into the wrong hands.

If you were to share a two-page term sheet about a proposed business partnership with a colleague and didn't want the term sheet to be distributed any further, you could give your colleague the term sheet to read in your office. When he was done you could take it back. While your colleague knows the term sheet's content, he doesn't have a copy that can be further distributed, either intentionally or accidentally. By contrast, if you e-mail the term sheet to him, he has a perfect copy that you can't get back.

Once information has been sent into the digital world, it is virtually impossible to pull it back or even to know all the places it will ultimately end up. This means that before sending an e-mail with sensitive business information, an employee should ask himself if he believes the recipient will keep the information confidential and use it only for its intended purpose.

Although businesses recognize the positive impact e-mail has on productivity, there is also growing awareness of the liability e-mail presents when read by competitors or by judges during litigation. Disney chairman Michael Eisner once told a group of students at the University of Southern California, "If anything will bring about the downfall of a company, it is blind copies of e-mails that should never have been sent."[3] Such concerns have prompted companies to consider using computer programs that control recipients' ability to access or further distribute e-mail. These programs typically allow the sender to prevent the recipient from performing tasks, such as saving, printing, or forwarding an e-mail. In addition, these programs encrypt e-mail messages so the sender can "delete" an e-mail after he has sent it. After the recipient gets an e-mail, he still has to request the key to decrypt it in order to read it. When the sender decides that a particular e-mail should never be read again, the e-mail's key is destroyed so it can never be decrypted again.

This kind of e-mail technology addresses a real corporate need to control the unbridled distribution of business information over the Internet. But before adopting this technology, a company should examine its effectiveness. In order to protect all of a company's e-mail, not only do all employees have to use modified e-mail programs that enforce these new protections, but every recipient does as well. While a company can require its employees to use modified e-mail programs, it has far less leverage to force other companies to modify theirs. Even if a company could mandate the use of this technology by all parties with whom its employees exchange business e-mail, the time and expense of its deployment would hinder the immediate electronic communication needed to pursue new business opportunities.

BUSINESS PARTNERS AND COLLABORATION RISKS

Every business that uses the Internet, even if only for e-mail, opens up its information assets to the risk of unauthorized access and use. Consider the trade exchange discussed in chapter 6 to understand why such environments necessitate a different approach to access control than the ones discussed so far. A company discloses information assets, such as product catalogs and price lists, when it becomes a member of an online trade exchange. Since this disclosure takes place during the registration process, a company has the opportunity to make explicit access control decisions about these information assets.

However, other information is disclosed in the course of using a trade exchange, and a company doesn't always have the opportunity to make access control decisions or even know that such decisions should be made. In particular, processing a transaction through an exchange results in the disclosure of information such as the trading partners involved, the items sold, per-unit cost, and total cost. A trade exchange or other trading partner could use this information for a number of purposes, including selling specific information, such as the amount of sheet metal a company has ordered for the next quarter, to competitors. Such information could then give a competitor valuable insight into a company's upcoming production output.

This situation illustrates how each of the participants within a collaborative business environment has competing business objectives and trust objectives, and companies should consider these objectives before joining. For example, trading partners want to prevent sensitive business information, such as the volume and cost of a purchase order, from falling into the hands of competitors. Therefore they have an interest in encrypting transactions so that only the buyer and seller can see them.

However, this encryption poses business challenges for the company hosting the exchange. Without the ability to see the contents of transactions, it can't base fees on transaction information, such as the dollar value of a purchase order; nor is it able to use or sell transaction information for other purposes.

In addition to misgivings over the disclosure of information assets to a trade exchange, companies have further concern over the protection of their information assets within the exchange. Many companies have different price lists or pricing arrangements for different customers. The disclosure of one customer's pricing information to another customer who pays higher prices could result in lost revenue if the company decides to lower this customer's prices or if the customer leaves. This means that controlling access to a company's information assets depends not only on its own access control policies, but on those of other companies as well. Depending on the security practices of others is particularly troublesome in environments like a trade exchange, where competitors are present.

To manage these kinds of collaborative risks, companies should draw upon their business, IT, legal, and information security resources. The IT and security staff should assess the threats to company information that would result from any sort of collaboration, and business managers who are responsible for this information should determine how the company could be impacted by inadequate security protections at other companies. With this information, the IT and security staff can develop a set of technical and procedural security measures that meet the business managers' trust requirements for their information assets. The legal representative can then draft an agreement that embodies these requirements and include the agreement in the rest of the negotiations that take place before starting the collaborative business relationship.

FINDING ACCESS CONTROL FUNCTIONALITY

So where does one look for access control functionality? The program or application that manages an information asset is usually the one that enforces access control over it. For example, a computer's operating system enforces an access control policy over the assets, such as files, that reside on the computer. An operating system can enforce a policy that only two people working on a project can write or change a report, while everyone else can read it. Enterprise applications, such as those for customer support, control access to the information assets they manage. An application that helps brokers manage their clients' accounts can enforce a policy that brokers are only permitted to view the accounts of their own clients and no one else's. In both the operating system and enterprise application situations, a company is usually limited to the access control features these programs have, so companies should make these features an important criterion when evaluating new software.

Because of this limitation, there will be cases where applications don't have the necessary features to support a company's policies for accessing information assets. To remember and manage these outstanding access control requirements, a company should add them to the information asset table (see table 7-1). "Other Required Security Technologies" is the last column in table 7-1 and is used to record any security technology that an information asset needs for its protection, but doesn't have. This could include encryption, different authentication evidence, or more fine-grained access control, as is shown in table 7-1.

In addition to operating systems and enterprise applications, a third type of access control enforcement consists of applications whose sole purpose is to enforce access controls and provide other security services across a company's whole IT infrastructure. This can be

TABLE 7-1

Information Asset Table: Other Required Security Technologies

Asset Name	Other Required Security Technologies
Term sheet for a corporate acquisition	None
Customer record	Access control to individual fields in customer record
Company phone book	None

particularly useful for companies that are trying to implement a comprehensive security infrastructure. One caveat for companies considering these applications is that they need to understand clearly what access control features these products have so they know what policies they can enforce.

The underlying security technology for virtually all access control functionality is an access control list (see box 7-1). While it's important for IT administrators to understand how to create and manage access control lists to enforce their companies' access control policies, it's more important for business managers to focus on developing access control policies that protect information assets while at the same time making them accessible to those with a legitimate purpose.

HOW ACME MANAGES ACCESS CONTROL

At the beginning of the access control phase of the corporate security process, the COO tells the team that there is no hard limit on the amount of time it spends on security analysis and configuring access controls in current applications. However, because ACME didn't meet its sales numbers the previous quarter, there is no money available for the purchase of new access control technology.

ACME's security team starts to determine the company's access control objectives by reviewing the current and available access control permissions contained in the information asset table. The team then interviews employees and their managers to determine the necessary information access permissions for major job functions, such as product manager or shipping clerk, within ACME. For example, because all of ACME's overseas shipments are sent FOB (freight on board) a shipping clerk needs to indicate when a shipment is loaded onto a truck at the warehouse.[4] In order to do this, the shipping clerk needs permission to update this field in the shipment's record in ACME's order fulfillment application.

With this type of information, IT administrators update each application's access control permissions to reflect the job function–based

Box 7-1 The Technology Behind Access Control

The primary security technology that operating systems and software applications use to enforce access control policies is an access control list (ACL). An access control list is a collection of records associated with every information asset a business wants to protect. Each of these records contains the name of a user—or role assigned to a group of users—and the type of access the user or role has for a particular piece of information. For example, one record for a sales report could dictate that a user named Bob is allowed to update it, while another record might state that only someone who has been assigned the sales-audit role can view it. Access control lists are created during the process (described earlier) of granting a user or role access permissions. When someone requests access to a piece of information, the ACL confirms whether the user or his assigned role is allowed to access it.

In the real world, a dinner reservation is the same as a record on an access control list. When you call to make a dinner reservation for Saturday night at 8 P.M., the maître d' checks to see if a table is available at that time; if it is, he writes your name in the reservation book. This is the equivalent of creating an ACL record. When your party arrives at the restaurant Saturday evening, the host or hostess checks to make sure that you have a reservation before escorting you to your table. This is the same verification process that happens when a computer checks an access control list before it gives a user the information she requested.

"Capabilities," a less common but still important technology, represent a different approach to enforcing access controls, in effect eliminating the second security check. A capability contains the same information as an ACL record, but it is packaged and given to a user to present when making requests for information. Some capabilities are stored in cookies, which are small files placed on users' computers. Capabilities function in the same way as gift certificates. If you buy a gift certificate for a friend, he can take it to a store and present it as payment. The only security check that takes place is verifying your payment before handing over the gift certificate. When your friend tries to pay for something, the gift certificate will be examined to ensure it is genuine, just as a capability is checked to ensure it is authentic.

Part of the appeal of capabilities is the simplicity of omitting a second security check. The only potential drawback is that businesses can't change their minds once they have given someone the capability to access an information asset. Just like using a gift certificate, once a person has a capability, he can use it. This is in contrast to access control lists, in which privileges can be revoked at any time.

policy. There are, however, situations where the available permissions don't support ACME's access control policies. One example is the order fulfillment application. It isn't set up to allow access to certain parts of a shipment record but not others. This means that the shipping clerk has permission to change any part of a shipment record, including its destination. Given that the security team doesn't have the budget to address this issue now, it makes an entry in the information asset table to indicate that the access control permissions that apply to this information asset are not capable of supporting ACME's access control policy.

In addition to these analysis and configuration tasks, the security group develops and publishes two new policies. The first one emphasizes the importance of protecting sensitive ACME information, especially in the context of e-mail, and is distributed to the entire company. The second policy addresses the procurement of new business applications and states that all new applications must have sufficient access control mechanisms to support ACME's access control policies. This policy is distributed to all managers with responsibility for procuring new applications, as well as the entire IT department.

The next task involves contacting the partner company that is jointly developing a motor with ACME's R&D department. ACME wants to assess the access controls and other security measures the partner company is using to protect ACME's proprietary information. If this assessment shows that the company is not providing adequate protection for ACME's information, then ACME will require the company to update its protections. ACME realizes that this assessment should take place at the beginning of a business relationship instead of in the middle, and so it adds conducting a security assessment to the set of due diligence tasks it will perform before starting any new business relationship.

ACME also revisits the issue of allowing the motor company's employees to access its engineering diagrams. Having created login accounts for the VPN and computer-aided-design application, the next step is defining the employees' access permissions. ACME ensures that the outside employees can only use the design application by adding a new firewall access control rule that prohibits these employees from accessing any other applications.

Then, ACME makes sure the motor company employees can access only the engineering diagrams that they are working on. ACME uses the same design application for all of its engineering projects and currently has access controls in place that allow the sharing of information between different projects. ACME wants to continue to encourage collaboration among its own employees, but not with motor company employees. To accomplish this, an administrator for the design application creates access control list records that give motor company employees access only to the engineering diagrams they need for this project.

To add an extra level of security, the administrator creates negative access control list (NACL) records to explicitly prevent the motor company employees from accessing any other engineering diagrams. In any access control system that supports granting permissions to roles or to groups of users, it can be difficult to know which individuals have permission to access an information asset. A NACL record avoids the danger in situations in which someone inadvertently gets access to an information object he should not have; for example, by being granted a role that is not an exact match with his responsibilities.

The final analysis task the security team performs at this point is determining which job functions within ACME require enforced separation of duties. One place where this is an issue is the accounts payable department. Managers in this department and the security team agree that no one should be able to both enter invoices into the system and then authorize payments. Unfortunately, the application ACME uses to automate these functions does not support static separation of duties and there is no alternative for enforcing this separation.

However, the application does have the capacity to audit invoices. This means that an IT security administrator could compare audit records for entering invoices with those for approving invoices to search for potential fraud. But using these audit records in this way raises the question of why anyone should believe the content of these records. They are created and stored in a computer, and changing information on a computer is notoriously easy to do and difficult to detect. Chapter 8 will examine what it takes to have trust in the information you see online.

Knowing What's Real
in Cyberspace

Each of the trust objectives described in the previous chapters focuses on a fundamental business activity about which companies need assurance, whether they're using computers and networks or not. A company needs to keep sensitive information and operations confidential so competitors can't take advantage of them. Unless companies know who the other parties are in a business relationship or transaction, they can't participate in any meaningful way. And companies need to control who has access to their information so that it doesn't fall into the wrong hands.

This chapter addresses the final trust objective, validating the authenticity of business information. In a paper-based world, companies use the physical integrity of documents as evidence of their authenticity and reliability. There are well-known technologies and procedures for detecting forgeries on documents such as contracts and receipts. Documents of particularly high value, such as checks, include a host of security features to protect against alteration and misuse. On the other hand, information inside a computer or traveling over the Internet can be changed in an instant, leaving no clue as to what the original information was or even that a change took place. To understand how and when to trust information, this chapter focuses on three business situations: receiving information on which a company will base business decisions and transactions, downloading enterprise and desktop applications for corporate use, and recording computer user activity for accountability and security enforcement.

WHAT INFORMATION CAN YOU TRUST?

In August 2000, an investor named Mark Jakob was in deep water. He had sold shares in the technology company Emulex that he had borrowed from his broker, expecting that the stock would go down in value. He intended to repurchase shares at a lower price to pay back the borrowed shares and pocket the difference between what he sold high and bought low. Unfortunately for Jakob, Emulex's stock went up instead of down, leaving him with a huge loss he couldn't pay back. As a result, he needed a way to make Emulex's stock drop, and fast.[1]

His solution was to distribute a fake press release that said Emulex had restated its quarterly earnings, its CEO had resigned, and that the company was under SEC investigation. Late at night on August 24, 2000, Jakob e-mailed the fake press release to Internet Wire, a news distribution service for corporate information. The wire service promptly sent the press release to Bloomberg and Comtex News. The release was then picked up by other financial news services, including CBS MarketWatch and CNBC. Over the span of sixteen minutes the next morning, investors traded 2.3 million Emulex shares and nearly $110 million of their money disappeared forever.[2] The incident caused long-term damage to Emulex's reputation and provoked a federal class-action suit against Internet Wire and Bloomberg.[3] All because of a single unverified source of information transmitted over the Internet.

How did this happen? Everyone, from Internet Wire to Bloomberg to CNBC and its day-trading viewers, trusted the accuracy and authenticity of a press release—without any basis for this trust. The trouble started with Internet Wire, which didn't validate the digital identity of the press release's sender. Jakob sent the e-mail from a Yahoo! account that he created in the name of a nonexistent employee at Emulex's PR firm. However, once Internet Wire distributed the press release, everyone assumed it was true. They trusted that Internet Wire would only distribute valid press releases, so there was no need for anyone else to validate it.

Businesspeople need to know two things in order to trust the information they receive through their computers. They need to know who sent it and that the information they receive is exactly the same as the information that was sent. These two requirements hold regardless of whether the source of the information is a fellow employee, a business partner, or a news service. But making sure that the information you receive meets those requirements isn't an easy task.

In some cases it is possible to validate critical information via alternate sources, such as business colleagues or print or broadcast media. In many situations, however, it isn't possible or practical to get outside confirmation, so companies need to understand the trust evidence required to validate information in a purely digital environment. Consider the case of an employee who gets a research report on a competitor via the Web, or a software application that receives a purchase order from a trade exchange Web site. To validate the information, the recipient needs trust evidence to verify who sent the information, and that it didn't change in transit. In this situation, security technology that is a part of all Web servers and browsers can provide the necessary trust evidence. Called secure sockets layer (SSL), this technology seals information in "envelopes" so that no one can see or change it. SSL does this by using a digital certificate to validate a Web site's identity, and then encrypting all of the messages sent between a browser and a Web site. The decision to use SSL and therefore protect downloaded information is made at the site, so a recipient needs to verify that SSL is being used. One way of doing this is by checking the Web site address displayed in a browser. If the address includes "https:", then SSL is in force; if the address contains "http:", then there is no protection.

It is also important to validate information sent via e-mail before acting on it. Without additional protection, anyone with access to any of the computers or network connections through which an e-mail message travels can change it. Encrypting e-mail using S/MIME provides evidence of the sender's identity by means of his digital certificate and provides evidence that the e-mail has not been changed by verifying the sender's digital signature on the e-mail.

A third scenario addresses documents that multiple recipients need to validate because, for instance, they do not trust that any prior recipients have adequately validated the information. In retrospect, this would have been appropriate in the Emulex case. The technical solution is the same as it was for the e-mail scenario—digital signatures. Anyone who has the sender's digital certificate can use it to validate the sender's signature, thus establishing the sender's identity and the document's integrity.

Other occasions when a company needs to validate incoming information are variants of these three scenarios, and the security technology that provides the trust evidence here can be used in those situations, as well. When a company knows the trust evidence it needs to validate incoming information, it also knows the trust evidence it must provide in order for other companies, government agencies, and individuals to validate information they receive from the company.

MAKING DOWNLOADS SAFER

Businesses increasingly download computer programs from the Internet. These programs range from small plug-ins that enhance Web browsing to enterprise applications that power the back-office and e-commerce operations of major corporations. The importance of verifying the source and integrity of downloaded programs is even more important than verifying information. With information, the recipient has the option of acting on it or not, and of verifying it through other sources. Programs are different because the person downloading an application from the Internet has no way of knowing what the program actually does. A person may know the advertised functions of the program, but he doesn't know if the program actually performs those functions or if it performs only those functions. A software vendor, for example, could insert a Trojan horse into an application. Named after the military ploy that resulted in the defeat of the ancient city of Troy, a Trojan horse program contains hidden code that can do serious damage to the computer where the download took place. For example, in addition to playing streaming video, a downloaded media player with a Trojan horse could upload all the files on an employee's laptop to a hacker's computer and then delete them from the laptop.

The second threat comes from someone changing a program while it is being downloaded. In 1995, the *New York Times* published an article that highlighted how easy it is to change a program while it is being shipped across the Internet.[4] The article was based on the work of four computer security experts at the University of California at Berkeley, who described how to exploit a flaw in the system used to move files from one computer to another.[5]

This system, called the Network File System, checks to see that a file is going to the right computer, but it doesn't check to see that the contents of a file are the same as when the file started its trip. The Berkeley security experts exploited this flaw to modify copies of the Netscape Web browser that passed through university computers while they were downloaded from Netscape to the users who requested them. They wrote a program that automatically changed the part of the browser program that generates the keys SSL uses to encrypt information, such as credit card numbers. Instead of generating new keys, the modified browsers always generated the same key, known only to the Berkeley foursome. This meant that they could decrypt all SSL communications with any of these modified browsers, and no one would be the wiser.

This is just one example of how someone can take advantage of a situation that continues to this day because the systems that transfer files across a campus, a company network, or the Internet don't check to see if anyone has changed the information along the way. Even in those cases where it's possible to check, this security functionality is almost never turned on.

Companies need the same trust evidence to validate programs as they do for documents. They need to know a program's source and that no changes were made to the program during transmission. However, because programs are generally much larger files than information such as a press release, not all of the same security technologies will apply. In particular, the manner in which browsers and Web sites communicate with each other is not efficient for transferring large files, such as those containing enterprise applications. This means that the SSL security functionality in browsers and Web sites is usually not a practical choice for protecting programs.

Digital signatures, on the other hand, can provide both types of trust evidence. After a software company digitally signs a program, anyone who has the company's digital certificate can then validate the signature. Often, a company's digital certificate accompanies the downloaded program; in other cases, it can be retrieved from a public directory, similar to a phone book.

Certificate authorities issue a special kind of certificate, often called a code signing certificate, specifically so companies and individuals can validate the programs they download. Before issuing a certificate, a certificate authority validates a requestor's identity, as was described in chapter 6. However, this process is still subject to human error. On January 30 and 31, 2001, the certificate authority VeriSign mistakenly issued two code signing digital certificates to a person posing as a Microsoft employee.[6] With these certificates, the impostor could have written programs that stole, corrupted, or destroyed personal and corporate information and then forged Microsoft's signature to distribute them. To anyone who attempted to validate these signatures, the programs would look like they were genuinely Microsoft's. VeriSign discovered the mistake about a month and a half later and, along with Microsoft, took action to prevent further use of the signing certificates.

But the damage was done. The possibility of issuing digital certificates to the wrong people has long been recognized, which is one of the reasons many financial institutions perform this task in-house. For them, the consequences of a third-party mistake are too high.

For many other companies and business situations, the risk is acceptable. Texas Instruments (TI), for example, outsourced the issuing and management of digital certificates for their customers, distributors, and suppliers to VeriSign. These TI partners can use their certificates to authenticate themselves to applications that let them order products and request confidential product information.[7]

RECORDING DIGITAL ACTIVITY

Another time at which companies need to assure themselves, and sometimes others, of the authenticity of digital information is when they are recording online activity. The specific activities a company needs to record vary according to a number of factors, such as a company's business practices, its industry, and government regulations. But there are a few general motivations that drive companies to record most of these activities. The first concerns holding individuals accountable for their actions. For example, when a manager approves travel expenses or vacation requests for one of his direct reports, it is important to the company, manager, and employee that there is a reliable record of this action, in case there is a dispute in the future.

A second motivation for recording the same activities is to verify that people are not abusing their privileges. The development and enforcement of a comprehensive access control policy, as outlined in chapter 7, goes a long way toward protecting business information and assets. However, access controls cannot prevent a person from misusing his privileges. A bank can use access controls to restrict the number of employees authorized to execute electronic fund transfers; however, access controls by themselves can't prevent an authorized employee from transferring funds to a personal account. The most effective and therefore most dangerous type of insider abuse takes place when the insider doesn't draw attention to himself because he never exceeds his permissions.

Another motivation for recording user actions is to detect attempts to bypass or subvert security protections, such as user authentication and access controls. For example, repeated failed logon attempts may indicate that a hacker is trying to guess an employee's password, and denied access requests can indicate that a user is trying to exceed his permissions.

The process of collecting this information is called auditing. The individual records are called audit records, and the collection of all audit records is called an audit trail. There are three requirements for auditing the types of activity described here:

- a unique digital identity for every user;

- the capability to audit the events a company wants; and

- a way of protecting both individual audit records and the audit trail.

Although requiring a unique digital identity seems obvious, there are a few common situations in which companies do not have unique digital identities for each user. The first instance is the use of anonymous administrative accounts, in which the username is just that, "administrator." Anonymity, coupled with the lack of access controls discussed in chapter 5, make administrative accounts particularly dangerous. If an enterprise application supports administrative roles, it is better to create unique accounts for all users and then grant the appropriate administrative roles to the employees who have these job functions. Guest accounts are another case in which users do not have a unique identity. These accounts allow someone limited use of a computer or application without having to go through the process of registration. Disabling these accounts is sound security practice.

As is frequently the case with user authentication and access control, operating systems and enterprise applications generally audit users' activities, such as logons and denied requests for information assets. It becomes a problem if the software doesn't include the functionality to audit all of the events a company needs. Most enterprise applications focus on auditing events that could indicate security violations, not on auditing actions for accountability. The applications that companies use limit their auditing capability just as they limit their level of access control. This is why one of the entries in the information asset table includes security functionality a company still needs, which can include enhanced auditing.

The final requirement for auditing user activity is protecting both individual audit records and the audit trail. This means that no one can add, change, or delete individual audit records or delete the audit trail. Since audit records often contain sensitive information, it is prudent to protect their confidentiality as well. Direct responsibility for protecting an audit trail is shared between the application performing the auditing and the operating system managing the application. The application is responsible for protecting the audit trail from its users, and the operating system is responsible for protecting the application, including its audit trail, from other users and applications on the computer.

Given the complexity of protecting traditional audit trails, there is some movement toward using digital signatures as another means of enforcing accountability. With this approach, the user who performs an action digitally signs the corresponding audit record instead of an application creating an audit record and adding it to an audit trail. Part of the reasoning behind this approach is that it's necessary to protect only private (signing) keys, not all audit records. And systems using digital certificates already address this issue.

As described previously in this chapter, the process of verifying a digital signature on an audit record will detect any changes to an audit record. However, any detected change to an audit record renders it useless as evidence. An attacker could effectively cover his tracks if he were able to change or corrupt the audit records he signed, or their signatures. This means that even if company applications start to use digital signatures to hold users accountable for their actions, it is still necessary for companies to protect the integrity of every audit record in addition to every signature.

WHAT SHOULD ACME TRUST?

In the final phase of ACME's corporate security process, the security team's mission is to minimize the company's risk from information and programs received or downloaded from the Internet and to increase employees' accountability for their actions. The team starts this process by interviewing a broad sample of employees to determine what information the company regularly receives via the Internet. They find the most common type of incoming information is e-mail. In addition, several departments receive reports from various industry analysts that address trends and make recommendations for companies in ACME's market. In addition, employees surf the Web for business news and for miscellaneous information.

The security team wants to assess the likelihood that ACME employees will make bad business decisions based on information that has been tampered with. One way the team gauges this risk is by examining the opportunities employees have to verify the information they receive. In the first two cases (e-mail and industry reports), employees can telephone the sender to verify any surprising or unusual information. In the case of business news, employees can make comparisons to coverage in other news media. In the case of miscellaneous information found on the Web, employees can verify it by using other sources. When the security team presents this analysis to senior management, one executive responds that the team's work in this regard is very thorough, but irrelevant. He goes on to say that ACME never makes a decision based on one piece of information, or even several pieces of information. The company bases its decisions on a large body of information, and so verifying every single piece of information that ACME receives via the Internet is not a priority.

With this in mind, the security team turns its focus to downloaded software. The team starts by looking at how ACME receives the enterprise software the IT department administers. They find that a little under half of the applications and maintenance releases are downloaded from the Internet; the rest are shipped on CD. The process of downloading applications includes some protection against accidental changes that can occur in the ordinary transfer of files over computer networks. However, none of the applications has any protection against deliberate tampering. At the security team's recommendation, ACME's head of software procurement calls each of these vendors to request that they ship their applications and maintenance releases on CD via an overnight delivery service.

To address the risk from programs downloaded by employees, ACME publishes a company policy prohibiting this practice and deploys Web proxy servers to enforce the policy. Web proxy servers serve as filters for all outgoing employee requests for Web pages and all incoming information and files, including program files, delivered in response to these requests. ACME sets up its proxy servers to prevent employees from downloading files that are obviously programs—for example, files whose names end in ".exe". The security team makes it clear that this approach is not foolproof, but will reduce ACME's vulnerability to malicious programs.

Moving on to accountability, the security team focuses on determining what user actions should be audited. The team interviews managers throughout the company about business or regulatory requirements for user accountability and about situations in which a user could misuse his legitimate access rights. Health care regulations governed by the U.S. Health Insurance Portability and Accountability Act (HIPAA) require companies to audit the actions of users who access employee records that include health care and insurance information.[8]

During this investigation the team discovers that the human resources application containing employee health insurance records does not meet HIPAA requirements. That application can only audit users' attempts to access employee records they're not authorized to see, not what they do with records for which they are authorized. ACME contacts the application vendor to find out when the required auditing capability will appear in the application. The vendor says this functionality will be in a release scheduled for general availability the following year. Given the vendor's history of slipped delivery dates, ACME explores migrating to a different HR application or service. At the same time, ACME's public policy director looks into the likelihood of further delays before HIPPA compliance is mandatory.

The last auditing issue the security team addresses is protecting the audit trail itself. The specific concerns are preventing anyone from deleting or changing the audit trail to cover their tracks and preventing unauthorized people from seeing sensitive information contained in the audit trail. This is a combined effort that starts with using an application's own access control features to limit access to its audit trail. Then the security team sets operating system access controls to protect the files containing an application's audit trail. Finally, the team proposes a combination of security technology and procedures to make offline backups of audit trails. As an immediate measure, ACME starts to store and protect audit trail backups separately from other backups, and in the near term, ACME will start to encrypt audit trail backups for additional protection.

SUMMARY

This chapter concludes the description of the technical components of the Trust Framework and the corporate security process. Most of the individual tasks can be completed in the order presented or in parallel, while others, such as security product selection, may depend on analysis performed later in the process before they can be finished. Still other measures, such as the use of security features upcoming in a new release of a company application, must wait until the upgrade is available.

Companies need to address the technical tasks discussed so far in order to protect themselves. However, a company won't be able to undertake the security process effectively without the necessary corporate support. Chapter 9 examines the organizational dynamics a company must navigate in order to benefit from the Trust Framework and the process described in this book.

NINE

Putting Your
Security Process
into Action

At this point, you've learned how to address your company's information security needs by focusing on your company, its information assets, and its business activities, not just its computers. You've learned to view information security from the perspective of establishing pervasive trust in your company, not as a collection of solutions that ward off known attacks. And you've learned the four trust objectives of conducting business and how companies can meet these objectives in the digital world through the use of information security technology.

However, a company will benefit from a new security perspective and strategy only if it can solve the management issues that arise from addressing information security in a comprehensive way. This chapter addresses these organizational issues, including getting and maintaining executive support for the security process, building the team that will do the work, and developing budgets and schedules.

GETTING EXECUTIVES INVOLVED

To understand and solve a company's information security problems, it's absolutely critical to have the necessary executive support to pay for and staff the effort. Even though the media is full of reports on cyber crime, and business and government leaders have proclaimed the critical importance of information security, it is still difficult to convince executives to write checks for it. There are several contributing factors, but one of the biggest is understanding the return on investment (ROI) for money spent on information security. The ROI is easy to understand in the case of virus protection because the loss a company suffers from a virus infection is obvious and easily calculated.

However, the ROI argument for a comprehensive program to protect a company's information assets and operations is a more difficult sell for executives. The first hurdle is the abstract and incomplete nature of the benefit. The argument that "if we spend X amount of money, our company will be more likely—but not guaranteed—to resist cyber attacks that could result in financial loss" is not particularly compelling. And then there is the opportunity cost. The money an executive allocates to information security is money he can't spend on improving sales for the next quarter. The specter of hacker threats isn't productive, either. I've seen numerous attempts to convince executives of the importance of information security at briefings that include examples of attacks, both real and imagined. At times engaging, these stories of potential attacks or attacks on others are not compelling.

The most persuasive argument focuses on eliminating current or imminent pain, either for a company as a whole or for individual executives. A devastating cyber attack is clearly a damaging event, but one that most companies don't think they'll suffer. A more compelling threat is lost customers and sales. One company hired me immediately after a potential customer, one of the largest banks in the world, said it would not become a customer until the company fixed its pervasively weak information security. The prospect of losing this customer—not to mention other business in the financial services market—caused sufficient distress that the CEO and his executive staff all supported a security project to close the sale to this customer and make the protection of customer information a competitive selling point.

Government regulations are another, more consistent form of pain. Businesses in highly regulated industries, such as financial services, can be closed down if they do not pass government audits of their information security technologies and procedures. The Gramm-Leach-Bliley Act raised the bar by requiring more stringent privacy protections for consumer financial information, and by raising the specter of personal executive responsibility for privacy violations.[1] Regulations that mandate information security protection aren't limited to financial services. Other industries such as health care face similar mandates from the Health Insurance Portability and Accountability Act. The European Union and individual countries, including the United Kingdom and Germany, have enacted privacy regulations that will have a direct impact on companies with international operations when they are consistently enforced.[2]

Regulations affect not only regulated companies, but also businesses that provide services for these companies. For example, one company that provides human resources services added security features, including encryption, to its applications because a *Fortune* 100 customer needed this level of protection to comply with government regulations. One element that all of these regulations have in common is that they can't be met solely through the use of the computer-oriented technologies such as virus protection software and firewalls. The Trust Framework provides companies with a helpful approach and structure for complying with these regulations—a prerequisite to play in many markets.

Some executives recognize the importance of information security to their companies without the immediate threat of government sanctions or lost customers. They generally work for companies that have a clear understanding of the value of their intellectual property and the lengths competitors will go to steal it. However, without such painful threats, most executives won't spend the time and money it takes to address security proactively and comprehensively.

ASSEMBLING THE SECURITY TEAM

Once executives have agreed in principle to move forward on a security program, they need to understand its scope in terms of staffing, budget, and timing. The specifics will vary from company to company, but the following guidelines hold across the board.

1. *Employees are your biggest allies.* Companies should use as many of their own employees as possible to create a security team, and the security team should engage as many employees as possible during its work. Not only will this help improve all employees' knowledge of security, it will also promote their acceptance of new security technologies and procedures, which is essential for their effectiveness. Companies will derive no long-term value from hiring a large team of consultants who carry out a corporate security review, write up their results, present the report, and leave.

2. *Education is as important as technology.* The function of the security team is to analyze and address a company's information security requirements in accordance with the security process described in this book. But no matter how effectively and efficiently a security team executes the process, companies will benefit only if information security is addressed throughout their organizations on an ongoing basis. This means that educating employees during the security process is as important to a company as, for example, selecting the right technology to authenticate users.

3. *It isn't just the IT department's responsibility.* The number of people on a security team will vary depending on the size of a

company, but it's crucial that the team represent a broad array of interests. In a small company, for example, the team could consist of the CEO, an attorney, and a technical support person. In a large, multinational company, the team could have a dozen executive sponsors and more than one hundred team members across the globe. In either case, there should be a core group that performs most of the work and an auxiliary group that provides support as needed. In addition, employees throughout a company, and at times employees of other companies, will provide information during the security process. One ground rule that helps ensure the valuable ongoing cooperation of these contributors is never to give them writing assignments. Core team members should be responsible for documenting all collected information; that way, it's sure to get done.

So, who should be on the team?

Core Team

1. *Security expert.* The security expert is the technical lead for the corporate security process and has overall responsibility for collecting and analyzing the information gathered and for the recommendations and plans that the team proposes. In addition, his responsibilities include educating team members and other employees, as needed, on information security technologies, policies, and best practices. This person should have a broad and deep understanding of information security technology and its application in business situations. Some companies will not have employees with the necessary experience, and so will hire a consultant for this role.

2. *Program manager.* The program manager has management responsibility for the security process, including tasks such as developing and tracking schedules, budgets, and all supporting projects. As the formal interface to the rest of the company, she

provides ongoing status reports and coordinates all security process deliverables. In addition, she is responsible for the creation and ongoing maintenance of tools, such as the information asset table, that will be used both during the security process and after the process has been completed. Ideally, the program manager should already know or be able to quickly identify all relevant stakeholders within the company.

3. *IT administrator.* The IT administrator has several major responsibilities. The first is documenting relevant information about a company's current information security situation. This includes identifying the operating systems and applications that manage a company's information assets and configuring their security features to provide the appropriate amount of protection for these assets. The second is setting up routine procedures, if ones don't already exist, for the computer-oriented protections described in chapter 3. The third is acting as liaison between the security team and the IT department during the planning and implementation phases for new security technologies. In all but the smallest companies, this role will be shared by a number of administrators, each addressing his or her own particular area of expertise, such as enterprise applications or configuring employee laptops. In these situations, one administrator will have additional responsibility for coordinating and ensuring the consistency of other administrators' tasks.

4. *Researchers.* Researchers gather most of the information during the security process. This task involves detective work because most companies have scant documentation on the security aspects of corporate policies, business roles, and responsibilities. Nor do they have much information about the security provisions in the applications employees use. Ideally, researchers have a strong familiarity with their company's information systems and business practices or, at minimum, an understanding of information systems and business practices

in general. While desirable, a strong security background is not necessary. The more experience researchers have, however, the more they will be able to operate independently of the security expert.

When drawing from its own employees, companies should look for researchers throughout their organizations. When possible, researchers should research their own departments. This reduces the amount of time it takes to come up to speed on departmental business issues and practices. Moreover, each of these researchers will bring greater understanding of security and their company's plans back to their departments.

Auxiliary Team

1. *Executive sponsor.* The executive sponsor is responsible for maintaining company support for the security process while it's under way and for eliminating any organizational roadblocks, such as a lack of cooperation from a department or office, that are impeding progress. Some amount of pushback is inevitable when people realize that they'll have to change some of their actions as a result of the security process.

2. *Strategic planner.* The strategic planner(s) and the security team discuss company strategy with two perspectives in mind. The first is ensuring that future company activities will have the necessary information security support. The second is exploring other company activities that would be possible with the right information security support.

3. *Business managers.* Business managers provide the security team with insight into how the company currently operates and how they think it *should* operate. In addition, they put security team members in touch with their employees for their perspectives. This input helps to ensure that the proposed security technologies and procedures will help and not hinder employees' work.

4. *Corporate counsel.* The corporate counsel advises the security team on relevant regulations and laws it needs to address. In addition, she is responsible for drafting and executing contracts relating to the security practices and performance of partner companies.

A client of mine that was seeking business in the banking industry set up its security team as follows. Overall management responsibility was assigned to the CIO. The CIO, who was directly involved in all decision making throughout the project, assigned day-to-day responsibility for scheduling, budgeting, intracompany coordination, and so forth to a project manager in the IT department. The project manager had experience in information security from a prior job, which proved helpful because he understood the dependencies between different tasks within the project.

In addition to the CIO and the project manager, the core team consisted of a senior security administrator in the IT department, several members of the development team for the application the bank would be using, and me. The VP of marketing, who contacted me to participate in this effort, had the most direct involvement in the project of any of the senior executives other than the CIO. This reflected the company's view that this effort was strategic and helped underscore the relationship between business objectives and security technologies.

Product managers and application developers from throughout the company briefed the team on current operations and future plans and helped with information gathering. Product groups within the company had a great deal of autonomy, and some of the security team's recommendations required changes in the way they operated and in their products. This meant that the core team had to spend a significant amount of time selling other parts of the company on the benefits of improved security.

Everyone on the core and auxiliary teams other than myself was a company employee. Having established work relationships throughout the company definitely helped the core team gather the information it needed. However, these established relationships were even more important when it came time for the company to start adopting the security team's recommendations.

BUDGETING AND SCHEDULING

The cost and duration of the information security process varies significantly from company to company, depending on factors such as the company's size and the complexity of its business operations. However, it's possible to break down the project into several phases and characterize the costs and duration associated with each. Figure 9-1 illustrates these phases.

1. Preliminary Steps

The first phase covers the time from a triggering event, such as a regulatory compliance review or hacker break-in, through getting executive approval and beginning the corporate security process. This phase consists of internal meetings and briefings to solicit and coordinate support for the effort. One company I advised reorganized parts of its IT and software development departments after getting executive approval but before starting the security process. The primary cost during this

FIGURE 9-1

Four Phases of the Corporate Security Process

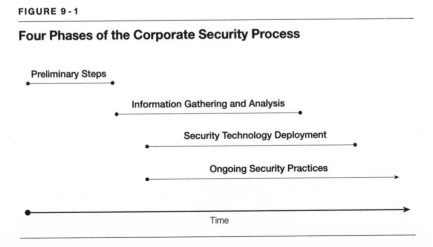

phase is employee time. It's important to complete this phase as quickly as possible or momentum will be lost, especially in cases where the pain of the triggering event fades.

2. Information Gathering and Analysis

The second phase begins with the identification of information assets and continues with the application of the Trust Framework to all of a company's digital business activities. The major factor affecting the duration of this phase is the time it takes to gather information about a company's business practices, information assets, corporate applications, and subversive access paths. Another factor is the time required to change current security settings, where needed. In setting the size of the security team, companies can minimize schedule or expense. A larger team may cost more, but the work may get done faster. Labor costs for the security team are the primary expense for this phase. This includes employees, who may be considered a sunk cost, and consultants, who are an explicit expense. The cost of determining subversive paths to information assets can be a surprise if this task is outsourced. Many security consulting firms offer vulnerability assessment services that essentially cover the tasks described in chapter 2. They charge upwards of $100,000 for a moderate-size company with approximately one thousand employees.

3. Security Technology Deployment

This phase begins with the first security product selection and includes the purchase, installation, and configuration of these products. One reason these activities make up a separate phase for planning purposes is that the primary expenses are for hardware and software, not labor. The hardware purchases may be for security-specific items such as firewalls, tokens, and smart cards, or for additional computers that will be used for security tasks, such as administration. Similarly, the software purchases will include a combination of security-specific programs, such as those for encrypting information, and enterprise applications that have the security features a company needs. A second reason for placing these activities in their own planning phase is that vendors and product availability have significant impact over the duration of this phase. It's difficult to estimate the cost of this phase before starting the previous phase because the amount and type of new security technologies can vary significantly from one company to the next. Companies do, however, have control over these costs through product selection and phased deployment.

4. Ongoing Security Practices

The last phase addresses recurring costs and activities arising from the corporate security process. Even though this phase starts during this process, it should be budgeted separately because these expenses will continue after the process has been completed.

Some activities will take place continuously or as needed. These include keeping virus definitions and the information asset table up to date, configuring firewalls, monitoring intrusions, and installing security upgrades. Other activities, such as revising security policy documents, scanning corporate networks for vulnerabilities, reviewing audit trails, and testing password strength, can be scheduled. The frequency with which a company undertakes these activities depends on the company's protection requirements as well as the amount of staff and money the company can apply to them.

THE ROLE OF POLICIES AND CONTRACTS

Information security technology is one important component in the protection of a company's information assets. However, without corresponding support from employees and executives, this technology alone can't protect a company. That's one reason many companies have security policies that define the roles and responsibilities of their employees regarding use of corporate computing resources.

Unfortunately, in many cases a company's employees never see their company's security policy. If they do, it appears to be comprised entirely of boilerplate material, irrelevant to them. The key to an effective security policy is to make it simple, relevant, realistic, and enforceable. Employees will be much more willing to abide by a security policy when they know the reasons behind the policy provisions and can clearly see how their actions contribute to the overall health of their company. In my own consulting practice, I have found it useful to give security policies an expiration date of three to four quarters after publication, and to include a section on proposed changes or additions to the next version of the policy. This helps avoid the all-too-common experience of a company spending a great deal of time developing rules or policies and coordinating approval throughout its organization, only to have the final policy documents gather dust in someone's bookcase or laptop.

A company's own employees aren't the only people who are affected by new security policies. As highlighted numerous times in this book, the security practices of other companies and their employees have a great impact on the security of one's own company. This means that companies need to include information security protection provisions in all third-party agreements where a third party's lack of security protections and procedures could harm the company. This entails identifying all of the business information that will be exchanged and defining the rules under which it will be used, shared, and protected.

The large bank referenced earlier in the chapter did precisely this during its negotiations with one of my clients. The bank knew what information security protections it needed and did not engage in a business relationship until they had been met. This need was emphasized by Bart Perkins, the chief information officer of Tricon Global Restaurants, a *Fortune* 300 company with over $22 billion in 2001 sales that owns Pizza Hut, Taco Bell, and Kentucky Fried Chicken. During a security panel at the University of Chicago Law School, Perkins said, "Business partnerships and alliances with suppliers and customers increase exposure to both security and privacy risks. IT security requirements should be explicitly spelled out in contracts between different companies."[3]

SECURITY IS A BUSINESS DECISION

For many, information security appears an impenetrable subject, understandable only by those with extensive technical skills. As a result, many corporate security decisions are made without the participation of the people responsible for a company's operations and growth. Without the input and understanding of executives familiar with all facets of a company's business, security solutions may not adequately protect a company and can even inhibit its growth.

However, today's emphasis on security widgets and computer-oriented protections doesn't give businesspeople the opportunity to apply their expertise and experience to this critical issue. What they need is a framework that puts a company's business and not its computers at the center of information security decision making. Companies need to approach information security from the angle of determining the protections they need to conduct their business activities and then look to security technologies as a means of providing that protection.

At this point, you've learned how a company can use this new perspective to address its current information security needs. Chapter 10 will cover the role information security technology plays in a company's future.

TEN

Transforming Your Business Through Information Security

After completing the corporate security process, how can you maintain the level of protection your company has achieved and adapt security technologies and policies as business activities change? The key is to apply the Trust Framework and what you've learned about trust objectives and trust evidence to all new and changing business situations. One use of the Trust Framework is to make sure the adoption of new technologies or business practices does not expose a company to new risks. For example, consider a company that wants to let its employees access enterprise applications from wireless personal digital assistants (PDAs) as well as from wired desktops and laptops. The introduction of PDAs and wireless technology means the company needs new security products—trust evidence—to authenticate its users' identities and protect the confidentiality and integrity of their transactions.

But you can do far more with your understanding of trust and protection than help your company enhance existing procedures. You can also discover ways in which information security technologies can change the way your company does business. This chapter will show how to apply what you've learned about protecting your company to the task of identifying and pursuing business innovation.

HOW SECURITY IMPACTS BUSINESS

One way of discovering how information security technology can promote innovation is to start by looking in the opposite direction, at how the security technologies companies use actually impose constraints on business activities.

Automated teller machines (ATMs) illustrate how the evidence used to meet trust objectives can either impose or eliminate constraints on transactions such as withdrawing cash. Because ATMs were introduced in the 1970s, you might think the technology is too old and the story too familiar to be relevant today. However, that's exactly the point. ATMs continue to be an innovative business device even today because of the way information security is used in their deployment. Their very familiarity makes it easy for us to forget the role security plays in each and every transaction.

A bank's trust objectives for routine banking include knowing who its customers are, making sure customers are able to access only their own funds, maintaining the confidentiality of financial information, and keeping transaction records to address fraud and reporting regulations. In a typical branch bank, meeting these objectives is labor-intensive. A teller verifies a customer's identity by validating authentication evidence such as a photo ID, signature, or passbook. Because tellers are the ones who hand over cash to customers, they enforce the restriction that customers can access only their own funds. Tellers are also the ones who enter transaction records into a bank's auditing system. In addition to teller discretion, the bank building, vault, and locked file cabinets help ensure the confidentiality of the bank's and customers' financial records.

What limitations does the trust evidence for banking with a teller impose, and what are the business consequences? The limitations are that simple banking transactions can take place only when a teller is present to authenticate customers, dispense cash, and enter transaction records, and these transactions can take place only within a physical bank. The consequences of these limitations include, among other things, long customer lines, the need to employ enough tellers, and the need for sufficient bank space to accommodate them all.

Next think of how the situation changed with the introduction of ATMs. Customers can withdraw money when and where it's convenient for them and banks can reduce operating expenses for staff and capital expenses for buildings, while at the same time expanding the number of customers they can service.

In order to accomplish this, banks need new trust evidence to satisfy their requirements for customer authentication, transaction confidentiality, and so on—evidence that doesn't impose the same limitations as in-person banking. This new trust evidence includes inserting ATM cards and entering PINs instead of presenting a driver's license to a teller, and using encryption to replace the privacy inherent in teller/customer exchanges. Even technologies that are not considered security-related are part of the trust evidence. Within an ATM, for instance, there is a small camera that photographs each bill and a sensor that checks the thickness of each bill before it dispenses cash. In addition to audit records of customer transactions, this evidence can be used in the event of a dispute over the cash an ATM dispensed. Non-security technologies, such as leased telephone lines and printers, are necessary for ATMs to work, but it is well-chosen security technologies that make ATMs a viable innovation for banks.

This example illustrates how the security mechanisms a company uses to protect itself can limit its business activities in terms of time (banking hours), location (a bank), and scale (number of customers and tellers), and how the use of security technologies can remove these limitations. It's important to note that existing security mechanisms do not necessarily make a business weaker or more vulnerable, but they do limit its ability to function optimally. The lesson for businesspeople is this: *If you want to find opportunities in which information security can promote innovation at your company, focus on removing limitations of time, location, and scale.*

USING SECURITY TECHNOLOGY FOR INNOVATION

With an idea of how security can limit business, let's turn to the ways security can enhance business. The process of pursuing innovation enabled by security technology can begin with a business activity, transaction, or situation that needs improvement, such as an under-utilized factory, high shipping expenses, or, in the case of ATMs, long lines at a bank. It can also begin with a business activity that seems fine, so fine that no one has bothered to examine it in years.

The first step is to look at the time, location, and scale limitations of a business activity. Ask questions, such as, When does the activity take place? Where are the participants during the activity? Where would they be otherwise? For global business activities, the when and where questions are directly linked. Look at the scale of an activity in quantifiable terms, such as income, expense, duration, and number of participants.

Now think about how you could improve on the business activity if these limitations didn't exist. How should your company conduct this activity? Play around with changing the activity's time, location, and scale characteristics, both larger and smaller. When you've come up with some innovative ideas for the activity, find out what is preventing you from implementing them. See if the trust evidence for the activity is part of problem, as tellers and bank buildings were in the ATM example. If it is, then look for alternative trust evidence that still meets your company's trust objectives, but doesn't impose any limitations on the activity. Chapters 5 through 8 explain how companies can use different security technologies, policies, and procedures to achieve the level of protection they need. Think of these as a set of tools you can use to improve the way your company does business.

IT'S ABOUT MORE THAN INTERNET SECURITY

The Internet provides numerous examples of innovation that are possible only with security technologies such as encryption and passwords. Because of the protection these technologies provide, a person can pay bills, buy groceries, or place a bid on a villa in Crete from her apartment in San Francisco. The Internet provides so many examples of innovation, in fact, that it's easy to think that it's the only place where information security is relevant.

The innovation possible through information security technology, however, is not limited to banking and Internet commerce. Security-enabled innovation can be found in places as disparate as your local movie theater and the racetrack. Think about how feature films are distributed to movie theaters. Traditionally, movie studios make multiple copies of their movies on 35-mm film and ship the film in canisters to theaters that have contracted to show them. According to industry analysts, the worldwide cost of distributing movies this way is more than $2 billion a year.[1] Within the nascent digital cinema field, studios are exploring new, less expensive ways of distributing movies, one of which is via satellite. Boeing Digital Cinema is one example of such a distribution service. A studio ships a digital master file of a movie to Boeing's Network Operation Center (NOC); from there it's transmitted to a satellite and then downloaded to movie theaters.

Given the movie industry's high degree of concern over piracy, one trust objective for movie distribution is keeping the content of a movie secret until it's projected in a theater. The evidence to establish that trust is based on the physical protection of film reels while they are being delivered. Encryption provides an alternative form of trust evidence for satellite distribution. In Boeing's system, the master file is encrypted for transport to the NOC and then for distribution via satellite to movie theaters. Within the first five months of operation, beginning in March 2002, more than ten thousand screenings of movies were distributed via Boeing's system. These included *Star Wars Episode II: Attack of the Clones, Spy Kids II, Signs,* and *The Banger Sisters.*[2]

This is an example of how the use of security technology as a form of trust evidence can remove limitations on how a business activity is conducted. With the protection encryption provides, the same movie could be distributed simultaneously to countless movie theaters around the world, with an estimated distribution cost savings of 75 percent.[3] In addition, this protected distribution channel could be used to deliver other content, such as sporting events or rock concerts. Granted, there are still technical, business, and logistical issues to be resolved before digital movie distribution enters the mass market, but without security technology, it's a nonstarter.

Another example of security-enabled innovation can be found at the Hong Kong Jockey Club, an organization with a clear business objective of making betting on horse races as easy as possible. It operates the Happy Valley racetrack on the island of Hong Kong and the Sha Tin racetrack in the New Territories, a half-hour subway ride to the north. On a typical race day there are more than seven million betting transactions and more than eight thousand betting staff assisting the Jockey Club's clientele.[4]

In an effort to make wagering more convenient, the Jockey Club allows Hong Kong residents to place bets from their cell phones. Given the amount of money at stake, this expansion of betting operations could be contemplated only if new security technologies replaced the protection offered by staff at the racetracks. To use this service, a prospective bettor can take his cell phone to one of five hundred telephone stores, where he presents evidence to prove his identity, age, and Hong Kong residency. After evaluating this documentation, the telephone store creates and loads digital certificates and private keys onto the SIM card inside his cell phone. A SIM (subscriber identity module) card is a smart card the size of a postage stamp that plugs into a cell phone. Once the registration process is complete, he can bet on horse races as well as transfer money between his bank account and his gambling account at the Jockey Club by pushing a few buttons on his cell phone. And he can do this anywhere he can get a signal. Digital signatures authenticate bets and funds transfers, and encryption ensures transaction confidentiality, according to Steve Beason, the Jockey Club's CIO.[5]

Extending betting services to mobile phones is part of the Jockey Club's strategy to provide more efficient, cashless transactions and to combat competition from online gambling, much of it illegal. The number of people placing bets through cell phones and other interactive devices increased by 27 percent from the 2000–2001 season to the 2001–2002 season.[6]

ISN'T THIS JUST TECHNOLOGY INNOVATION?

The capacity of information security to eliminate barriers that restrain business innovation may seem too familiar and therefore ring false. After all, isn't removing limitations on time, location, and scope one of the promises of the Internet and the so-called New Economy? Books such as *How Digital Is Your Business: Creating the Company of the Future* and *Net Ready: Strategies for Success in the E-conomy* already provide thorough guidance on the business strategies companies need to adopt in order to survive and grow in today's business environment.[7] Information security technology doesn't figure prominently in these strategies. Actually, there is barely a reference; and a survey of other, well-respected books on the subject will reveal the same situation.

So what is information security's contribution to business growth and innovation? How is it relevant? The answer depends on a company's attitude toward corporate responsibility and the assumption of risk, and can be summarized by the thought that just because you can do something, doesn't mean you should. Just because you can drive a Porsche 911 over 190 miles per hour through city streets at 3:00 A.M. doesn't mean you should. Or that you'll survive. Information security technology and establishing trust in your business operations are relevant to innovation only if you plan on a second trip.

Pursuing innovation by eliminating limitations of time, location, and scale without understanding which limitations are consequences of a company's current protection mechanisms puts a company at risk, a risk that is unknown and therefore can't be managed. Further, such uninformed activity can put a company's investors, customers, and partners at risk without their knowledge.

I recently encountered an example of this kind of risky innovation at a prominent software vendor that sells enterprise applications, including one that companies can use to track customers and sales leads.[8] The information contained within this particular application can provide a clear picture of a company's sales and therefore its financial prospects. Users can connect to this application over the Internet from their laptops to retrieve and update their customer and sales information. The software vendor added encryption to the application to protect this sensitive information while it travels over the Internet and added other security technologies that it highlighted in its marketing literature. So far, so good.

The software vendor, wanting to eliminate the location limitation of having to be near a telephone or network jack, released a product that enables users to access the application and its information from a wireless PDA. However, in the move to a wireless network, the software vendor didn't replace the encryption it used to protect sensitive information in transit. In fact, the software vendor didn't replace most of the security technology it had used. The consequences are that anyone who picks up a user's PDA can view and change any of the information the user can. Anyone with a wireless laptop in the vicinity of a user can intercept all of the customer information he is viewing or updating. And with a small bit of work, a hacker can impersonate a user and access all of a user's information, even if the hacker doesn't have the user's PDA.

This scenario shows that even if you are moving from one way of doing business to another, you still need to ensure that you don't undermine the security protection you depend on.

I asked one of the software developers who worked on this product why the company hadn't included security technology to protect their customers' information. His reply: Security wasn't their responsibility. In fact, this developer was already aware of the security vulnerabilities described here. He wasn't able to explain why his company incorporated appropriate security into its wired product but not the wireless one, and acknowledged that customers might incorrectly assume that the wireless product offers the same protections as the wired product.

The attitude that security is someone else's problem, or is something to be addressed after the real work gets done, is pervasive in the business world. And it leads to the perception that security concerns just slow down innovation. For a fiscally responsible company, information security plays two parts in business innovation. One is a supporting role to ensure that any business innovation is planned and adopted in a way that protects the company and its stakeholders. The other is a leading role in driving innovation by eliminating operational constraints imposed by previous protection measures.

WHAT THE FUTURE HOLDS

What can the future hold for business if it broadens its interest in information security and trust from protecting the here and now to building for the future? Let's start to answer this question by returning to the film distribution example in this book's introduction and see what innovation is taking place today and what is possible today. From there we'll take a look at what is possible tomorrow.

In the introduction, I highlighted a scenario in which film production companies, with the correct security, could use the Internet to distribute dailies, or the results of the day's filming, to anyone who needed to see them, anywhere in the world. It is standard practice on many movie location shoots for a crew member to board a plane at the end of every day's filming to hand-carry the undeveloped dailies back to the studio for processing and distribution, according to Louis Eales, the director of cinema products at Dolby Laboratories.[9] (Dolby develops audio technology that is used throughout the movie industry.) The need to hand-deliver movie clips is not uncommon either, and on one occasion filming stopped entirely so Eales could fly a segment of film to an executive for review. In these and many other similar situations, the level of protection movie studios required for these film clips was nothing less than an employee courier.

Now it is an increasingly common practice to use pairs of cameras when filming. One is a traditional camera that uses film that will go into the final print; the other is a digital camera that is mounted to take exactly the same pictures as the traditional camera. The output of the digital camera replaces traditional dailies; it can be viewed instantly on the set and can be distributed electronically, provided the necessary protection exists. Some progress is being made in providing this protection. According to Eales, the dailies for a recent movie filmed in New Zealand were sent over the Internet to a studio in Los Angeles. There was an encryption device on location and one at the studio, so dailies were protected in transit. This obviously represents real improvement over trans-Pacific flights and is an adequate solution—if everyone who needs to see the dailies is in the studio.

However, it's seldom the case that everyone is actually in the studio, and so the filmmakers have to revert to overnight delivery for those who aren't on site. The problem with this part digital/part analog solution is that it focuses on delivery to a place, not a person. It starts down the path of eliminating location limitations, but doesn't go far enough. The next step in this innovative progression would be to deliver dailies to the people who need them, regardless of where they are. The individual security technologies required to accomplish this, such as encryption optimized for wireless networks, are all commercially available. All that remains is for them to be packaged together for easy use.

What could happen tomorrow? It would seem at this point that we've exhausted the elimination of location limitations as a source of business innovation, at least until interplanetary business trips are routine. However, there is still another location limitation to look at, the one between a person and his computer. A businessperson can travel around the globe and work any time of the day or night, but he can't perform certain activities without *his* computer. His computer has the files and applications he needs; it is the context of his work life. For the occasional task, such as checking flight schedules, he can use a public computer, but not for his real work, not for work that involves sensitive business matters. For an employee to be fully productive he needs to have his computer and the information on it. Businesspeople lug their laptops around all the time, so what's the problem? Well, carrying laptops everywhere we go is one of the problems. The other is that we sometimes decide to leave a laptop at the office, and then wish we hadn't.

So, let's move to a model where people rent laptops on business trips, much the same way they rent cars. Unlike rental cars, the rental laptop will for all intents and purposes be the same as the laptop or desktop that was left at the office. It will be like a rental car that has already matched your seat adjustments, has preset the radio stations to play the same music you listen to in your own car, and has your skiing equipment in the trunk. And once you return the car, all of this disappears so the next renter has no idea you were ever there.

What does it take to do this? All of the security technologies necessary to accomplish this have already been discussed in this book, but some assembly is required. You have to start with a laptop that already has the applications and general information that a businessperson would need, but has nothing specific to anyone. When a person rents a laptop, he inserts a smart card and enters a password to authenticate himself to the rental laptop network to which his company belongs. At this point, the core set of applications and data he needs is downloaded from his company through this network to the laptop. Among other things, this will include all of his e-mail and files relating to the current business trip and all of his personal settings. This download takes place over an encrypted network connection (wired or wireless), and the information he gets is based on an access control decision made using his smart card–stored digital identity. As he works, all of the additional information he needs will be downloaded in the same fashion. When he returns the laptop and removes his smart card, the laptop goes through an induced "amnesia" so everything specific to that user is erased. The rent-a-laptop company can even offer premium amnesia services so that someone with an electron microscope wouldn't be able to find any residual information.

With this system a traveling movie studio executive can view dailies anywhere in the world and on any available computer—and we have eliminated another limitation on business.

Personalized rental laptops are just one example of innovation that is possible when you apply the Trust Framework to all new business situations. Thinking about your company's future in these terms doesn't require any special training or security background. There will always be someone who can explain the detailed technical issues involved. What you need is a new way of thinking about security—based on trust—that will survive the changing threats and technologies ahead.

Business Encryption Overview

With the advent of the World Wide Web in the mid-1990s, encryption emerged from the world of government secrets and now plays an integral role in protecting business information and transactions. This appendix introduces the major types of encryption that companies use to protect the confidentiality and integrity of business information, to authenticate users, and to enforce accountability. In practice, all of the encryption steps described in this appendix are performed by software and not by people.

SYMMETRIC ENCRYPTION

Symmetric, or conventional, encryption has been used for thousands of years. Until the 1970s, it was the only kind of encryption that existed in the world. The method is called symmetric because the same key is used for both encrypting and decrypting information.

A simple way to grasp the idea is to think about the cardboard decoder toy that you got in a cereal box when you were a child. It had two concentric rings, one smaller than the other, and the alphabet was printed on each of the rings. The inner ring rotated so the A on the outside ring could be lined up with any letter on the inside ring.

When you wanted to send secret messages during school, you would pick a letter, for example *D,* and then align the inner *D* with the outer *A* on each of the decoder toys. To encrypt each letter in a message, you would go to the letter on the outer ring and then write down the corresponding letter on the inner ring. For example, *DOG* encrypts to *GRJ.* To decrypt each letter in a secret message, you reverse the process and go to the letter on the inner ring and write down the corresponding letter on the outer ring.

This childhood example is similar to using symmetric encryption to ensure the confidentiality of business information. Everyone with whom you share encrypted information needs to use both the same encryption algorithm and the same key. In the example, the encryption algorithm was the two-alphabet decoder toy and the key was the letter *D.* In today's digital world, encryption algorithms are based on complex mathematics and are implemented most commonly as computer programs.[1] Encryption keys are long numbers.

Key distribution for symmetric encryption has long been a problem because it's not safe to distribute keys over the same network or infrastructure that you use for sending encrypted messages. Keys are therefore distributed "out of band," such as through armed couriers, Federal Express, and the telephone. These approaches are labor-intensive, expensive, and don't scale well to accommodate a large number of users. They also pose the logistical requirement of having compatible encryption devices. This was easy to accomplish with decoder rings because everyone could carry the same decoder toys. However, if you want to exchange encrypted messages with a business colleague, both of you need access to computers with compatible encryption programs installed. This may not be a problem if you only use your own computers. The situation becomes more difficult, and at times impossible, if you use computers that are not your own, such as PCs in hotel business centers, cyber cafés, or other public places.

Two of the most common symmetric encryption algorithms in use today are the Data Encryption Standard (DES) and RC4. DES is used extensively worldwide and was developed in 1975 by IBM for the National Institute of Standards and Technology (NIST),[2] with input from the National Security Agency (NSA). RC4 is used for encrypting communications between browsers and Web sites on the Internet. Other well-known symmetric encryption algorithms are IDEA (International Data Encryption Algorithm) and Blowfish.

In 2001, the U.S. government concluded a multiyear international competition to choose a successor to DES. The winner was a Belgian algorithm named Rijndael (pronounced "Rhine-Doll"), which will be widely used for many years to come.

PUBLIC KEY ENCRYPTION

Unlike symmetric encryption, public key encryption has only been around since 1976, when Whitfield Diffie and Martin Hellman, two researchers at Stanford University, published a paper describing it.[3] Instead of using a single key to both encrypt and decrypt information, public key encryption uses two keys: a public key and a private key. Together these keys are called a "key pair."

Whatever is encrypted with one key can be decrypted only by the other key in the pair. As the names suggest, private keys should be kept secret, but public keys are widely available through online directories that function much like phone books.

Sending a message to a colleague using symmetric encryption requires first finding a secure, out-of-band means of sending the encryption key so the colleague can decrypt and read the message. With public key encryption, you encrypt a message with your colleague's public key and then send it. Since your colleague is the only one with his corresponding private key, he is the only one who can decrypt and read the message.

Public key encryption operations are much slower than symmetric key operations because of the mathematical calculations involved, so it is impractical to encrypt large messages or reports with a public key.

A more efficient approach is to encrypt the message with a symmetric key, encrypt the symmetric key with a colleague's public key, and then send both the encrypted key and encrypted information to the colleague.[4] In this case, the colleague will first decrypt the symmetric key with his private key and then decrypt the message with the just-decrypted symmetric key.

The most common public key encryption algorithms being used today are

- RSA,

- Diffie-Hellman,

- Elliptic Curve Cryptography (ECC), and

- Digital Signature Standard (DSS).

MESSAGE DIGESTS

Message digest algorithms, also referred to as "hash functions," differ from symmetric and public key encryption algorithms in that they don't use keys. Message digest algorithms take any digital input, such as a word processing document or graphic, perform numerous calculations on it, and return with a unique number, commonly 128 bits or 160 bits long, that represents that input. That number is called a message digest. If you calculate a message digest on a different document, you get a new unique message digest. In neither case will you be able to figure out the contents of the original document from its message digest. The capability to encrypt something that can never be decrypted doesn't seem particularly useful if you are trying to communicate with a colleague. However, it's useful if you want to prove to others that you had information at a specific point in time without letting them know what the information was.

One occasion when message digests can be useful is an online auction, where there is a concern about insider fraud. In this situation, an insider working for the organization hosting the auction could read

the bids and then tell one of the bidders the value of bids already submitted, thus rigging the auction. One simple way of preventing this is
to have each bidder e-mail a message digest of their bid and not the bid
itself. Since the original bid cannot be derived from the message digest, it is impossible for an insider to know the value of any bid while
the bidding is still open. Once the bidding is closed, all the bidders
e-mail their actual bids; then new message digests are calculated and
compared against the ones already submitted. If they are equal, the bid
is valid; otherwise, the bid and the bidder are disqualified.

The two most popular message digest algorithms are MD5 (Message Digest 5) and SHA-1 (Secure Hash Algorithm).

DIGITAL SIGNATURES

Digital signatures are based on the "key pair" idea, which dictates that
what is encrypted with one key can only be decrypted with the other
key. Digital signatures allow you to encrypt a message with your private key, while allowing anyone with your public key to decrypt the
message. Since you are the only one with access to your private key,
you're the only one who can encrypt a memo with it. This is the signature process. Since your public key is available to the public, anyone
can decrypt the memo and verify the signature.

One shortcoming of this particular approach is that it's not efficient, because public key encryption operations are slow and the process
of signing a large document can therefore be quite time-consuming.
Message digests are often used to address this performance issue. Instead of encrypting the document, you first calculate a message digest
on the document and then encrypt the message digest.

The encrypted message digest is the digital signature. Verifying a
digital signature involves several steps. The first is decrypting the message digest with your public key. The second step is calculating a new
message digest on the original document. The third step is comparing
the two message digests. If they are equal, people know that you signed
the document and that no changes were made to the document after

you signed it. If the two message digests don't match, it means that either you didn't sign the document or it was changed after you signed it.

Digital signatures allow people to trust that your messages indeed originated from you. But if someone else has access to your private key, he will be able to digitally sign documents as if he were you. It's impossible to distinguish between a real signature and this forgery. The two most common digital signature algorithms are RSA and the Digital Signature Algorithm (DSA).

APPENDIX B

Corporate Security Process

Corporate Security Process

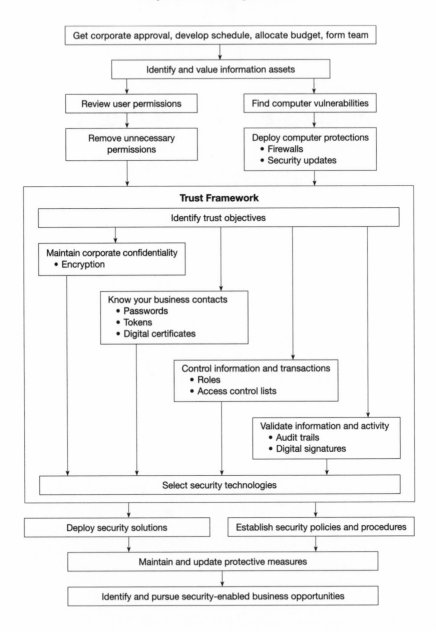

Get corporate approval, develop schedule, allocate budget, form team

Identify and value information assets

Review user permissions

Find computer vulnerabilities

Remove unnecessary permissions

Deploy computer protections
- Firewalls
- Security updates

Trust Framework

Identify trust objectives

Maintain corporate confidentiality
- Encryption

Know your business contacts
- Passwords
- Tokens
- Digital certificates

Control information and transactions
- Roles
- Access control lists

Validate information and activity
- Audit trails
- Digital signatures

Select security technologies

Deploy security solutions

Establish security policies and procedures

Maintain and update protective measures

Identify and pursue security-enabled business opportunities

NOTES

Introduction

1. "Windows 32 Viruses Rule the Waves," Sophos corporate Web site, <http://www.sophos.com/pressoffice/pressrel/uk/20020701sixmthtopten.html> (accessed 9 September 2002).

2. Chet Dembeck, "E-Commerce Sites Crippled by Hacker Sabotage," February 9, 2000, <http://www.newsfactor.com/perl/story/2466.html> (accessed 9 September 2002). And, Sen. Patrick Leahy, "Statement of Senator Patrick Leahy, Ranking Member, Senate Committee on the Judiciary, Joint Senate-House Hearing on 'Internet Denial of Service Attacks and the Federal Response,'" Patrick Leahy Web site, 29 February 2000, <http://leahy.senate.gov/press/200002/000229b.html> (accessed 10 September 2002).

3. Louise Levathes, *When China Ruled the Seas* (New York: Oxford University Press, 1994).

Chapter 3

1. Carolyn Duffy Marsan, "Is the Internet Shrinking? Nonsense!" *Network World*, 28 January 2002, <http://www.nwfusion.com/news/2002/0128 notshrinking.html> (accessed 12 September 2002).

2. This type of firewall functionality is referred to as *packet filtering*.

3. This firewall functionality is called *stateful inspection*.

4. This type of firewall is called an *application proxy*.

Chapter 4

1. *The American Heritage Dictionary of the English Language*, 4th ed., Great Books Online, 2000, <http://www.bartleby.com/61/97/S0209700.html> (accessed 9 December 2002).

Chapter 5

1. John Schwartz, "As Wireless Networks Grow, So Do Security Fears," *New York Times,* 19 August 2001.

2. Safeware, The Insurance Agency, "2001 Loss Statistics Charts," <http://www.safeware.com/losscharts.htm> (accessed 26 August 2002).

3. "CPSR Gives Norbert Wiener Award to Phil Zimmermann," Computer Professionals for Social Responsibility, 22 August 1996, <http://www.cpsr.org/issues/zimm.html> (accessed 26 August 2002).

4. "Digital Cell Phone Crypto Cracked," *Wired News,* 20 March 1997, <http://www.wired.com/news/topstories/0,1287,2676,00.html> (accessed 12 September 2002).

5. Yoshiko Hara and Junko Yoshida, "Code Hack Prompts Delay of DVD-Audio Launch," *EE Times,* 3 December 1999, <http://www.eetimes.com/story/OEG19991202S0046> (accessed 12 September 2002).

6. MIT Distribution Center for PGP (Pretty Good Privacy), <http://Web.mit.edu/network/pgp.html> (accessed 26 August 2002).

7. S/MIME Central, <http://www.rsasecurity.com/standards/smime/index.html> (accessed 26 August 2002).

8. Transparent Key Management™ is an alternative encryption technology, which may be used to protect the sensitive business information ACME shares with the partner motor company. Transparent Key Management imposes no security responsibilities on users, requires minimal administrative support, and can be deployed quickly. (*See* International Patent Publication WO 02/43317 and U.S. Patent Publication 2002/0064283.)

Chapter 6

1. A preferred approach is to temporarily lock an account after a series of failed login attempts. This eliminates a potential "denial of service" attack in which an attacker deliberately enters invalid passwords so the legitimate account holder won't be able to authenticate himself without assistance from an administrator.

2. Andy Briney, "A Smart Card for Everyone?" *Information Security,* March 2002, <http://www.infosecuritymag.com/2002/mar/cover.shtml> (accessed 27 August 2002).

3. Sharon Walsh, "Oprah, Call Your Broker," *The Industry Standard,* 2 April 2001, <http://www.thestandard.com/article/display/0,1151,23031,00.html?nl=dnt> (accessed 8 April 2002).

4. Patrick Thibodeau, "FTC Vows to Keep Closer Tabs on Privacy Breaches," *Computerworld,* 11 June 2002, <http://www.idg.net/crd_idg search_879493.html> (accessed 14 September 2002).

5. Jim Kerstetter, "You're Only as Good as Your Password," *BusinessWeek*, 23 August 2002, <http://www.businessweek.com/smallbiz/content/aug2002/sb20020823_5482.htm> (accessed 27 August 2002).

Chapter 7

1. David Ferraiolo and Richard Kuhn, "Role-Based Access Controls," National Institute of Standards and Technology, 16 October 1992, <http://hissa.ncsl.nist.gov/rbac/paper/rbac1.html> (accessed 3 September 2002).

2. "Anatomy of a Scam," *Asiaweek*, 25 August 1995, <http://www.asiaweek.com/asiaweek/95/0825/biz1.html> (accessed 3 September 2002).

3. Thomas W. Hazlett, "Tattletale Email," Forbes.com, 21 August 2000, <http://www.forbes.com/asap/2000/0821/194.html> (accessed 3 September 2002).

4. When a company ships a product FOB, its responsibility for the product ends the moment it's put on board the shipping transit service.

Chapter 8

1. Thom Mrozek, "Emulex Hoaxer Indicted for Using Bogus Press Release and Internet Service to Drive Down Price on Stock," U.S. Department of Justice, 28 September 2000, <http://www.usdoj.gov/criminal/cybercrime/emulex.htm> (accessed 16 April 2002).

2. "Jakob: Go to Jail," *Wired News*, 6 August 2001, <http://www.wired.com/news/business/0,1367,45849,00.html> (accessed 16 April 2002).

3. "Class Action Suit Filed Against Internet Wire and Bloomberg over Emulex Hoax," *Tech Law Journal*, 5 September 2000, <http://www.techlawjournal.com/seclaw/20000905.asp> (accessed 16 April 2002).

4. John Markoff, "Discovery of Internet Flaws Is Setback for On-Line Trade," *New York Times*, 11 October 1995.

5. Eric Brewer, Paul Gauthier, Ian Goldberg, and David Wagner were the computer security experts who exposed the flaw. And, Eric Brewer et al., "Basic Flaws in Internet Security and Commerce," University of California, Berkeley, <http://www.cs.berkeley.edu/~daw/papers/endpoint-security.html> (accessed 29 April 2002).

6. Robert Lemos, "Microsoft Warns of Hijacked Certificates," Cnet News.Com, 22 March 2001, <http://news.com.com/2100-1001-254586.html?legacy=cnet&tag=tp_pr> (accessed 8 October 2001).

7. "Texas Instruments: Controlled Extranet Access Saves Time and Improves Order Accuracy," <http://www.verisign.com/rsc/cs/ti_casestudy.pdf> (accessed 11 December 2002).

8. Centers for Medicare and Medicaid Services, "The Health Insurance

Portability and Accountability Act of 1996," <http://cms.hhs.gov/hipaa/> (accessed 15 September 2002).

Chapter 9

1. U.S. Senate Committee on Banking, Housing, and Urban Affairs, "Information Regarding the Gramm-Leach-Bliley Act of 1999," <http://www.senate.gov/~banking/conf/> (accessed 9 September 2002).

2. The European Union's Directive on Data Privacy was effective in 1998; the United Kingdom and Germany enacted data protection acts in 2000 and 2001, respectively.

3. Kathleen Melymuka, "Panel: Better Privacy and Security Require 'Cultural Evolution,'" *Computerworld*, 20 July 2001, <http://www.computerworld.com/securitytopics/security/story/0,10801,62411,00.html> (accessed 9 September 2002).

Chapter 10

1. "Boeing Digital Cinema Backgrounder," <http://www.boeing.com/defense-space/space/cinema/backgrounder/backgrounder.html> (accessed 11 December 2002).

2. "Boeing Digital Cinema Surpasses 10,000 Screenings, Demonstrates Live Streaming Capability," <http://www.boeing.com/defense-space/space/cinema/cinema_press/2002_10_31_screenings.html> (accessed 15 December 2002).

3. "Boeing Digital Cinema Backgrounder," <http://www.boeing.com/defense-space/space/cinema/backgrounder/backgrounder.html> (accessed 11 December 2002).

4. "Betting and Entertainment Highlights," <http://www.hongkongjockeyclub.com/english/about_hkjc/highlights_betting.htm> (accessed 15 December 2002).

5. Steve Beason, conversation with author, 29 July 2001.

6. "Betting and Entertainment Highlights," <http://www.hongkongjockeyclub.com/english/about_hkjc/highlights_betting.htm> (accessed 15 December 2002).

7. Hartman, Amir, John Sifonis, and John Kador, *Net Ready: Strategies for Success in the E-conomy* (New York: McGraw-Hill, 2000); Slywotzky, Adrian J. and David Morrison, *How Digital Is Your Business: Creating the Company of the Future* (New York: Crown Publishers, 2000).

8. I have changed various characteristics of this software company, for whom I've never consulted, and its product to hide its identity.

9. Louis Eales, telephone conversation with author, 9 December 2002.

Appendix A

1. Encryption algorithms are sometimes implemented in hardware, such as integrated circuits or smart cards.

2. At the time, it was called the National Bureau of Standards (NBS).

3. Whitfield Diffie and Martin E. Hellman, "New Directions in Cryptography," *IEEE Transactions on Information Theory* 10, no. 6 (1976): 644–654.

4. This combination of encrypted information and encrypted symmetric key is sometimes called an RSA digital envelope.

GLOSSARY

Access control   The process of preventing unauthorized access to information assets, in accordance with an access control policy.

Access control list   A list associated with an information asset that specifies the types of access users and collections of users have for that asset.

Access control policy   A policy that defines the set of legitimate access permissions for information assets; it may also include access permissions that are explicitly disallowed.

Algorithm   A set of instructions for manipulating data, often used in the context of an encryption algorithm.

Audit trail   A collection of records that describe user activity; these records usually describe security-relevant user activities, such as logging on to an application, or business-relevant activities, such as issuing a purchase order.

Authentication   The process of verifying a person's digital identity; for example, when logging on to a computer.

Back door   A secret way of bypassing security protections to access a computer or application.

Biometric   An observable physical characteristic, such as a fingerprint, retina, or voice pattern, that is used to authenticate a user.

Cryptography   See *encryption*.

Denial of service   Actions that monopolize computing services, such as a Web site, so that legitimate users are unable to use them.

Digital certificate   The digital world's equivalent of a passport; it attests to the identity of someone or something. An organization called a certificate authority issues a digital certificate after performing a set of checks to validate the holder's identity.

Digital identity   Something that represents a real-world entity, such as a person, to a computer or computer application. Login names and digital certificates are two examples.

Digital signature   An encryption process that can be used to verify the originator of a piece of information and that the information hasn't been changed.

Encryption   The process of scrambling data so that it becomes very difficult to understand. Data that has been encrypted is called cipher text. Cipher text that has been decrypted is called plain text. Data that has not yet been encrypted is also called plain text.

Firewall   A system consisting of hardware and/or software that erects a boundary between two or more networks. Often one of the networks is the Internet.

Information asset table   A table containing security-relevant information about a company's information assets that helps a company protect and manage those assets.

Key   A random number that is used to encrypt or decrypt information.

Message digest algorithm   An encryption process that transforms information into a unique number that can be used to increase the speed of calculating and verifying digital signatures. Once encrypted, a message digest cannot be reversed.

Public key encryption   A type of encryption that utilizes pairs of keys, one called a public key and the other a private key, such that anything encrypted with one key can be decrypted only by the other key.

Secure sockets layer (SSL)   A feature of Web browsers and Web servers that encrypts and digitally signs all of the information sent between the browsers and servers. SSL also authenticates Web servers via their digital certificates. User authentication based on digital signatures is optional.

Security policy   The collection of policies and procedures that define the roles and responsibilities of everyone within a company with regard to the protection of information assets.

Smart card   Often the same size and shape as a traditional credit card, a smart card includes a microprocessor and can be used to store encryption keys and perform encryption operations, as well as contain information about its owner.

Sniffer   A program that can intercept data as it travels across a computer network. Hackers use sniffers to capture sensitive information, including passwords.

Symmetric encryption   A type of encryption where the same key is used for both encrypting and decrypting information.

Token A security device that can be used as evidence when authenticating a user. One example is a token that generates a one-time password.

Trojan horse A program that ostensibly performs a useful function, but contains additional functionality that can perform unauthorized and damaging operations.

Virtual private network (VPN) A combination of encryption and other security mechanisms that creates a confidential link between two computers that communicate over the Internet. Data that passes through a VPN is protected, making it unnecessary for each application that uses the VPN to provide its own encryption.

Virus A program that has the ability to reproduce and distribute itself, and can damage files on the computers it infects.

BIBLIOGRAPHY

The American Heritage Dictionary of the English Language. 4th ed. Great Books Online, 2000. <http://www.bartleby.com/61/97/S0209700.html> (accessed 9 December 2002).

Boeing Corporation. "Boeing Digital Cinema Backgrounder." <http://www. boeing.com/defense-space/space/cinema/backgrounder/backgrounder. html> (accessed 11 December 2002).

Boeing Corporation. "Boeing Digital Cinema Surpasses 10,000 Screenings, Demonstrates Live Streaming Capability." <http://www.boeing.com/de fense-space/space/cinema/cinema_press/2002_10_31_screenings.html> (accessed 15 December 2002).

Brewer, Eric, et al. "Basic Flaws in Internet Security and Commerce." University of California at Berkeley. <http://www.cs.berkeley.edu/~daw/papers/ endpoint-security.html> (accessed 29 April 2002).

Briney, Andy. "A Smart Card for Everyone?" *Information Security.* March 2002. <http://www.infosecuritymag.com/2002/mar/cover.shtml> (accessed 27 August 2002).

Centers for Medicare and Medicaid Services. "The Health Insurance Portability and Accountability Act of 1996." <http://cms.hhs.gov/hipaa/> (accessed 15 September 2002).

Christensen, Clayton M. *The Innovator's Dilemma: When New Technologies Cause Great Firms to Fail.* Boston: Harvard Business School Press, 1997.

Computer Professionals for Social Responsibility. "CPSR Gives Norbert Wiener Award to Phil Zimmermann." 22 August 1996. <http://www. cpsr.org/issues/zimm.html> (accessed 26 August 2002).

Dembeck, Chet. "E-Commerce Sites Crippled by Hacker Sabotage." 9 February 2000. <http://www.newsfactor.com/perl/story/2466.html> (accessed 9 September 2002).

Diffie, Whitfield, and Martin E. Hellman. "New Directions in Cryptography." *IEEE Transactions on Information Theory* 10, no. 6 (1976).

Ferraiolo, David, and Richard Kuhn. "Role-Based Access Controls." National Institute of Standards and Technology. 16 October 1992. <http://hissa.ncsl.nist.gov/rbac/paper/rbac1.html> (accessed 3 September 2002).

Hara, Yoshiko, and Junko Yoshida. "Code Hack Prompts Delay of DVD-Audio Launch." *EE Times*. 3 December 1999. <http://www.eetimes.com/story/OEG19991202S0046> (accessed 12 September 2002).

Hartman, Amir, John Sifonis, and John Kador. *Net Ready: Strategies for Success in the E-conomy*. New York: McGraw-Hill, 2000.

Hazlett, Thomas W. "Tattletale Email." Forbes.com. 21 August 2000. <http://www.forbes.com/asap/2000/0821/194.html> (accessed 3 September 2002).

Hong Kong Jockey Club. "Betting and Entertainment Highlights." <http://www.hongkongjockeyclub.com/english/about_hkjc/highlights_betting.htm> (accessed 15 December 2002).

Kerstetter, Jim. "You're Only as Good as Your Password." *BusinessWeek*. 23 August 2002. <http://www.businessweek.com/smallbiz/content/aug2002/sb20020823_5482.htm> (accessed 27 August 2002).

Leahy, Patrick. "Statement of Senator Patrick Leahy, Ranking Member, Senate Committee on the Judiciary, Joint Senate-House Hearing on 'Internet Denial of Service Attacks and the Federal Response.'" Patrick Leahy Web site. 29 February 2000. <http://leahy.senate.gov/press/200002/000229b.html> (accessed 10 September 2002).

Lemos, Robert. "Microsoft Warns of Hijacked Certificates." Cnet News.Com. 22 March 2001. <http://news.com.com/2100-1001-254586.html?legacy=cnet&tag=tp_pr> (accessed 8 October 2001).

Levathes, Louise. *When China Ruled the Seas*. New York: Oxford University Press, 1994.

Markoff, John. "Discovery of Internet Flaws Is Setback for On-Line Trade." *New York Times*. 11 October 1995.

Marsan, Carolyn Duffy. "Is the Internet Shrinking? Nonsense!" *Network World*. 28 January 2002. <http://www.nwfusion.com/news/2002/0128notshrinking.html> (accessed 12 September 2002).

Melymuka, Kathleen. "Panel: Better Privacy and Security Require 'Cultural Evolution.'" *Computerworld*. 20 July 2001. <http://www.computerworld.com/securitytopics/security/story/0,10801,62411,00.html> (accessed 9 September 2002).

MIT Distribution Center for PGP (Pretty Good Privacy). <http://web.mit.edu/network/pgp.html> (accessed 26 August 2002).

Mrozek, Thom. "Emulex Hoaxer Indicted for Using Bogus Press Release and Internet Service to Drive Down Price on Stock." U.S. Department of

Justice. 28 September 2000. <http://www.usdoj.gov/criminal/cybercrime/emulex.htm> (accessed 16 April 2002).

Pfleeger, Charles, and Shari Pfleeger. *Security in Computing.* 3rd ed. Upper Saddle River, NJ: Prentice Hall, 2002.

RSA Security. S/MIME Central. <http://www.rsasecurity.com/standards/smime/index.html> (accessed 26 August 2002).

Safeware, The Insurance Agency. "2001 Loss Statistics Charts." <http://www.safeware.com/losscharts.htm> (accessed 26 August 2002).

Schneier, Bruce. *Applied Cryptography: Protocols, Algorithms, and Source Code in C.* 2nd ed. New York: Wiley, 1996.

Schwartz, John. "As Wireless Networks Grow, So Do Security Fears." *New York Times.* 19 August 2001.

Sophos Corporation. "Windows 32 Viruses Rule the Waves." Sophos corporate Web site. <http://www.sophos.com/pressoffice/pressrel/uk/20020701sixmthtopten.html> (accessed 9 September 2002).

Tech Law Journal. "Class Action Suit Filed Against Internet Wire and Bloomberg over Emulex Hoax." *Tech Law Journal.* 5 September 2000. <http://www.techlawjournal.com/seclaw/20000905.asp> (accessed 16 April 2002).

Thibodeau, Patrick. "FTC Vows to Keep Closer Tabs on Privacy Breaches." *Computerworld.* 11 June 2002. <http://www.idg.net/crd_idgsearch_879493.html> (accessed 14 September 2002).

Time Asia. "Anatomy of a Scam." *Asiaweek.* 25 August 1995. <http://www.asiaweek.com/asiaweek/95/0825/biz1.html> (accessed 3 September 2002).

U.S. Senate Committee on Banking, Housing, and Urban Affairs. "Information Regarding the Gramm-Leach-Bliley Act of 1999." <http://www.senate.gov/~banking/conf/> (accessed 9 September 2002).

VeriSign Corporation. "Texas Instruments: Controlled Extranet Access Saves Time and Improves Order Accuracy." <http://www.verisign.com/rsc/cs/ti_casestudy.pdf> (accessed 11 December 2002).

Walsh, Sharon. "Oprah, Call Your Broker." *The Industry Standard.* 2 April 2001. <http://www.thestandard.com/article/display/0,1151,23031,00.html?nl=dnt> (accessed 8 April 2002).

Wired News. "Digital Cell Phone Crypto Cracked." *Wired News.* 20 March 1997. <http://www.wired.com/news/technology/0,1282,2676,00.html> (accessed 12 September 2002).

Wired News. "Jakob: Go to Jail." *Wired News.* 6 August 2001. <http://www.wired.com/news/business/0,1367,45849,00.html> (accessed 16 April 2002).

RECOMMENDED READINGS

Each of the recommended readings listed here provides excellent treatment of the security technologies and concepts discussed in this book. Each one contains the most comprehensive handling of its subject matter and so offers the interested reader a wealth of information in a single package. *Security in Computing* provides a technical overview of the computer security field and treats the associated privacy, legal, and ethical issues as well. As its name suggests, *Applied Cryptography* covers encryption and its use. *Counter Hack* describes the tools and techniques hackers use to break into computers as well as the ways to get them out and keep them out.

Pfleeger, Charles, and Shari Pfleeger. *Security in Computing.* 3rd ed. Upper Saddle River, NJ: Prentice Hall, 2002.

Schneier, Bruce. *Applied Cryptography: Protocols, Algorithms, and Source Code in C.* 2nd ed. New York: Wiley, 1996.

Skoudis, Ed. *Counter Hack: A Step-by-Step Guide to Computer Attacks and Effective Defenses.* Upper Saddle River, NJ: Prentice Hall, 2002.

INDEX

ABOUT THE AUTHOR

THOMAS J. PARENTY is founder and President of Parenty Consulting, LLC (www.parenty.com). His consulting practice addresses information security and privacy needs in both the public and private sectors. He has focused on the security design and architecture of national and global systems, including those for banking, health care, and nuclear command and control. Parenty has been active in the information security and cryptography fields for twenty years, including his employment at the National Security Agency. He has testified five times before the United States Congress, advised the Presidential Commission on Critical Infrastructure Protection, and was a member of the National Research Council panel evaluating the National Institute of Standards and Technology's information security activities.

Parenty is a graduate of the College of the Holy Cross, where he earned his A.B. in philosophy. He received his M.S. in computer science from the University of Massachusetts at Amherst. He can be reached at tom@parenty.com.